THE EUROPEAN NOVELISTS SERIES

Edited by Herbert Van Thal

DOSTOIEVSKY

DOSTOIEVSKY

C. M. WOODHOUSE

ARTHUR BARKER LIMITED
5 WINSLEY STREET LONDON WI

Printed in Great Britain by
Lowe & Brydone (Printers) Ltd., London

CONTENTS

PREFACE

"I SPIT me of Sovietsky," said the bearded Russian to the ladies of Wood Hills Literary and Debating Society.[1] "P. G. Wodehouse and Tolstoy not bad," he added ; and there he expressed a point of view which might have seemed less heterodox in Moscow than in Wood Hills. For Tolstoy can be read with comfort by those who have been brought up to prefer the Western European style of novel, among them perhaps many Russians. So can Turgenev, whose country gentlemen would have been perfectly at home at Blandings ; and even Gogol and Goncharov describe Russians as we English expect them to be, however unlike ourselves. But Dostoievsky (whom a simple emendation is enough to identify with Sovietsky) is quite another matter : his novels, if they can be called novels, are like nothing on earth.

To read either Tolstoy or Turgenev in translation is to move in much the same climate as that of Jane Austen or Thackeray or even P. G. Wodehouse. For Tolstoy and Turgenev belonged to the landed aristocracy, whose way of life and thought had a fundamental uniformity all over Europe during the nineteenth century, and even into the twentieth. But Dostoievsky did not, and he bitterly resented it. According to the quaint system invented by Peter the Great, which enriched Russia with fourteen degrees of nobility, Dostoievsky was technically of noble blood ; but by upbringing and habit of thought he belonged to the lower ranks of the professional classes, and even they would have been glad enough during most of his life to disembarrass themselves of so barbarous and eccentric a specimen. His

[1] P. G. Wodehouse, *The Clicking of Cuthbert* p. 23.

climate of thought is entirely foreign to the average novel-reader of Western Europe. At first sight he is almost unintelligible even in translation. It is hardly surprising that many English readers, and some Russians whose national pride was sensitive to Western criticism, felt inclined to spit them of Dostoievsky when they first became aware of his work.

It is perhaps generally true, and certainly of my own case, that the first reading of any of Dostoievsky's works leaves a chaotic and disappointing impression. Some of them turn out not even to be worth a second reading ; but in the more important cases, the second reading begins to bring out the shape of a masterpiece, even if it has to be left to the third or fourth reading to bring the impression as near as is humanly possible to completeness. In other words, Dostoievsky's novels make harder reading than most, but the ultimate reward is incomparably more satisfying. The purpose of this book is to try to help newcomers over some of the earlier obstacles ; but the last part of the course can only be completed alone. My disqualifications for writing about Dostoievsky are too formidable to be enumerated. My single qualification is that Dostoievsky is the one novelist in the world whom I have found it worth an intellectual struggle to understand.

Some of the disqualifications have been overcome for me by others. No foreign writer has ever had a better translator than Mrs. Constance Garnett, whose translations of Dostoievsky's fiction were first published by Messrs. William Heinemann during the first world war, and republished after the second.[1] Few writers' lives have been the subject of such careful and thorough research, the results of which can to-day

---

[1] Except where otherwise stated, references and quotations in the text are taken from the new standard edition, by generous permission of the publisher.

very largely be taken for granted.[1]   There is consequently
almost nothing new in this book : it is a simple summary
of the known events of Dostoievsky's life (Chapters I–IV)
followed by a rather less simple attempt to relate that life to
his work and thought (Chapters V–VI).   I can only hope
that it will not have the same effect on the ordinary reader
as the bearded Russian had on the ladies of Wood Hills
Literary and Debating Society, which was to divert their
enthusiasm from Russian literature to golf.

[1] See the Select Bibliography, pp. 109–10. · Certain works to which
repeated reference is made in the text are given abbreviated titles, which
are explained in the bibliography.

CHAPTER I

PROMISE

DOSTOIEVSKY gave many clear hints in his writings about the right way to set about his biography. He was at one with Christ and Socrates in holding that the external events of a man's physical life were of little significance in comparison with the inner history of his spirit. "Life is everywhere life, life in ourselves, not in what is outside us," he wrote within a few hours of the greatest crisis of his life ; [1] and everywhere he stressed this distinction, both through the characters of his novels and in his own letters and diaries. It is his spiritual life, then, that a biographer should try to write, not neglecting the external events but accepting them rather as a reflection of the internal than as having an importance of their own. This balance, too, rests on Dostoievsky's own advice : [2]

> The external ought to balance the internal. Otherwise, in the absence of external impressions the internal acquires too dangerous a supremacy.

In his own case there are two reasons why the public events of his life cannot be entirely dismissed as irrelevant to those private to himself. One is that he was an intensely auto-biographical writer, so that his novels themselves cannot be understood without reference to his external life. The other is that for the earlier half of his life there would be nothing whatever to record if the external events were to be dismissed ; for his spiritual awakening came late. There is no writer of

[1] Letter to his brother Mihail, 22 December 1849 (Kotelianksy, p. 6).
[2] Letter to his brother Mihail, 1847 (Carr, p. 36).

whom it is more true that his life has to be seen as a whole to be comprehended at all. He lived almost sixty years ; and if he had lived two-thirds of that time, he would have left nothing that would ever have been read outside his native language, for it was only in his fortieth year that he produced a book which raised him above the average standards of his day. Before that he wrote much that was mediocre and some rubbish ; but the first forty years (literally as well as proverbially the worst) must be struggled through if only to show the long and agonising process by which the strangest genius of the nineteenth century reached maturity.

He was born on 30 October 1821 at the Marinsky Hospital in Moscow, where his father was a staff doctor ; he was christened Fyodor Mihailovitch. He was the second of seven children, the eldest being Mihail, and the others in order Varvara, Andrey, Vera, Nicholas and Alexandra. There is nothing of importance, or even of outstanding interest to Dostoievsky's biography, about this large family. They were chiefly proud of their " nobility," which Russian convention conferred on them by virtue of the father's position ; and although socially this meant no more than that they belonged to the professional middle classes, an attempt was even made to prove a connection with the Lithuanian aristocracy, which is almost certainly fictitious. The father was bad-tempered, niggardly, jealously suspicious, a stern disciplinarian, a dipsomaniac in his later years, but sufficiently well educated to be able to teach his boys Latin by himself ; the mother was gently self-effacing ; both were dead before Dostoievsky came of age. Having almost no other playmates in his childhood, he was dependent entirely on his brothers and sisters for company. Of them Mihail became by far his closest friend, but he was by no means the only member of the family who felt entitled to become financially dependent on Dostoievsky in his later days.

This undistinguished foreground of family gloom and austerity was perhaps of less importance to Dostoievsky's development than its geographical setting. He was by birth a Muscovite; but quite soon after he became independent he adopted Petersburg, the rival capital, as the home to which his spiritual roots belonged, and thereafter practically no scene in his published works can be found that is laid in the capital of his birth. The contrast between Moscow and Petersburg in the nineteenth century was as sharp and as fundamental as if they were in foreign countries, so that in transferring his roots from the one to the other Dostoievsky was deliberately taking a decisive step, changing from an intolerable to a congenial climate. Symbolically, he was escaping from prison : and that was evidently how he thought of the Moscow of his youth from the moment he became aware of Petersburg.

Even within the world of Moscow, the Dostoievsky children's lives were so circumscribed that they were brought up in seeming unawareness of its place in the contemporary world. The great poet Pushkin, Russia's ideally Byronic aristocrat, was at his prime in the Moscow of the 1820's ; the " spacious and lavish world where the aristocracy and landed gentry lived in careless luxury " [1] was at its zenith ; the " Decabrist plot " of the Liberal nobility against the Tsar Nicholas I, in December 1825, took place when Dostoievsky was four years old : but Dr. Mihail Dostoievsky, for all his noble blood, had nothing to do with these splendid affairs. Until 1830 the children scarcely left the austere hospital except to make an annual pilgrimage to a monastery some fifty miles away. Then, at last, in Dostoievsky's tenth year, his father was able to afford the purchase of a small farm in the province of Tula, and there at least for the summer months the children were able to enjoy a country life.

[1] Carr, p. 14.

The experience hardly turned Dostoievsky into a country boy. Nine-tenths of all his written work in later life was based in town-life, even if the background changed from Moscow to Petersburg ; and his attempts to portray peasants were always artificial. None is more artificial, or less likely to be based on fact, than the story which began as a vague reminiscence of an episode in childhood, no doubt at the farm in Tula, and ended as a carefully reconstructed short story for the delectation of child-psychologists.[1] This is the story of Dostoievsky's fright by an imaginary wolf, when he was soothed by a peasant who reassured him that there was no wolf, and " put out his thick, black-nailed, earth-stained finger and softly touched my twitching lips." In telling this story, Dostoievsky admitted that in his youth he was " subject to hallucinations, which passed away later." It is almost the only thing we know about his childhood at first hand, though his younger brother Andrey, in reminiscences written long afterwards, ascribes to him an affection for peasants. But it was, and always remained, the affection of a townsman who did not live among them or wish to do so.

The constricting atmosphere of drab puritanism, in which most of the year was passed at Moscow, was unrelieved even by any redeeming breadth of education. Apart from the doctor's Latin lessons (which had to be taken standing at attention), the children's reading was mainly confined to the Bible and the popular history of Russia by Karamzin, until the two elder boys were sent to a private day school kept by a Frenchman called Souchard, naturalised as a Russian under the supposedly anagrammatic name of Drashusov, and later to a private boarding school kept by a man called Chermak, which they attended from 1834 to 1837. The impression Dostoievsky formed of this experience can be deduced from a novel written with obviously autobiographical

[1] *The Peasant Marey* (1876), in the volume called *An Honest Thief*, etc.

intent a generation later.[1] It is clear that he hated school as
much as his father's Latin lessons. He was lonely, introspective,
poor and miserable, comforted only by the companionship
of his elder brother. The end of this unhappy first period of
his schooling coincided with the death of his mother after a
short illness in 1837. At the same time all Moscow was
ringing with the news of Pushkin's death in a duel, and it
appears from the memoirs of Andrey Dostoievsky that this
event moved his elder brothers even more than their domestic
afflictions. The symbolic coincidence marked the end of
Dostoievsky's childhood.

From Dostoievsky's reaction to the coincidence of private
and public tragedy (on which Andrey records that " his elder
brother several times said that, if we had not had our family
mourning, he would have asked father's permission to wear
mourning for Pushkin ") it is obvious that three years at
school had at least served to awaken his literary susceptibilities,
even if only at a superficial level, and even if this had little
to do with his formal education. He had begun to read
widely, but not deeply, among the romantic writers then in
vogue : Scott, Dickens, Balzac, George Sand, Schiller, Hugo,
Hoffmann, and of course Shakespeare. This phase persisted
during the years following 1837, when he entered the Military
Engineering Academy at Petersburg and so escaped from the
environment of Moscow for the first time. His father had
intended that Mihail also should enter the same career, and
sent them to Petersburg together ; but to Dostoievsky's
bitter sorrow his brother was rejected as medically unfit.
He was therefore alone for the first time in his life at the
age of sixteen, so that reading became naturally his one
consolation.

His external life continued to be no happier in the Academy
at Petersburg than it had been at home or at school. He had

[1] *A Raw Youth* (1875).

no pocket-money, he desperately missed his brother, and he felt no vocation for the career that had been chosen for him. His unhappiness is painfully evident in a letter written to his father : [1]

> Can you really think that your son is asking too much when he applies to you for an allowance ? . . . But I want to consider your difficulties, and so I will give up tea altogether, and ask you only for the barest necessity of all—sixteen roubles for two pairs of ordinary boots. . . . I dare not insist upon my petition : I am not asking too much, but my gratitude will be boundless.

The one personal consolation of the period is mentioned in another letter : his father, it appears, had sent his greetings to a young man called Shidlovsky through his two sons on their first departure to Petersburg, and Dostoievsky apologises for having failed to deliver them. It is not known how the father knew Shidlovsky, and certainly the elder son was unable to pursue the introduction far, because after failing to enter the Military Engineering Academy at Petersburg, he was admitted some months later to that at Reval ; but to Dostoievsky himself, Shidlovsky became for some time the closest friend and fiercest passion of his life. Shidlovsky was a romantic and attractive wastrel, who fitted well into the imaginary world which the adolescent Dostoievsky had constructed for himself out of his readings from Scott and Pushkin. But the passion was neither serious nor lasting, and it was soon replaced by another for an anonymous fellow-student who fitted still better into a new dream based on readings from Schiller. From the few letters which build up these alternations of ecstasy and despair, the only significant conclusion that emerges is that Dostoievsky was a very ordinary young man.

It is characteristic of his mentality at this date that when

[1] Mayne, pp. 1-3.

something truly unusual happened to him for the first time, he joined with the rest of the family in a conspiracy of silence about it which lasted all his life. In the summer of 1839, when Dostoievsky had been in the Military Engineering Academy a year and a half, his father was murdered by peasants on his farm. There is no allusion to the circumstances of the death in Dostoievsky's letters at the time, though of course he refers to the fact of it in writing to Mihail. Because in his last novel the father of *The Brothers Karamazov* is also murdered, it has been suggested that the character is based on Dostoievsky's father ; but the suggestion shows a complete disregard of Dostoievsky's method of portraiture from life. Old Karamazov was a lecherous and revolting villain of inspired turpitude ; old Dostoievsky was a hack by comparison, whose worst fault apart from drink and unfeeling sternness was extreme eccentricity. It is said that while his daughters were still in their teens, he used to search under their beds every night for concealed lovers ; and this foible is attributed by Dostoievsky not to old Karamazov but to another character in another book.[1] It is perhaps impossible to extricate any clear representation of his father from Dostoievsky's works. We only know that he greatly feared him and hardly missed him ; and of the murder, no member of the Dostoievsky family spoke openly at all, until the novelist's daughter published a biography of her father in 1921.

Dostoievsky's own reaction to the event was purely materialistic, though by no means selfish. He regarded the younger members of the family as destitute orphans. In spite of his own habit of reckless extravagance, he was prepared throughout his life to accept them all as financially dependent on himself. When they grew up, they were not slow to take advantage of his generosity, which several of them extended to their own dependents. Nevertheless, there was

[1] A drunken buffoon called Lebedyev in *The Idiot*, p. 190.

a certain income from the estate of the father, and there were considerable expectations from a wealthy uncle by marriage called Kumanin (the husband of a sister of Dostoievsky's mother). These circumstances gave Dostoievsky an unexpected opportunity to indulge in his three favourite occupations of the time—indolence, extravagance and generosity. He even began to think of writing, while still engaged on working for his military commission.

In 1843 he secured his commission and an appointment in the Engineering Department of the Ministry of War. Mihail took a similar commission and a German wife about the same time. The younger brother Andrey came to share a flat in Petersburg with Dostoievsky in the same year. A German doctor called Riesenkampf, who knew them all at this time, described with horror the financial disorder of the brothers' way of life, which culminated in Dostoievsky's decision in 1844 to compound the rest of his share in his father's estate for a sum of 500 roubles down and 500 a month thereafter. He resigned his commission in the same year. In these circumstances he began to look upon his literary ambitions in a new light : it was no longer a matter of romantic dilettantism, but of bread and butter. The prospect was by no means hopeless at such a period of literary ferment in Russia, where new journals pullulated annually ; but his wealthy uncle Kumanin advised him " not to be led away by Shakespeare, who was of no more use than a soap-bubble." [1]

His first literary efforts were as unoriginal as the rest of his life hitherto. He tried to complete someone else's novel called *Matilda* ; he translated Balzac's *Eugénie Grandet* into Russian ; he probably wrote at least one play ; he collaborated with his brother Mihail in a number of translations from Schiller. Of all these efforts not a word survives, and it

[1] Carr, p. 28.

cannot be said to be a pity. It is only interesting to know who were the first masters of his adult work. Schiller's name recurs constantly in all his work, chiefly as a symbol of romantic futility on the lips of sarcastic and unattractive characters. This is not a sign that Dostoievsky was profoundly impressed by his influence; rather the contrary. But of the influence of Balzac, whom he rarely mentions, there can be no doubt. Balzac shares with Gogol, Russia's first major novelist in point of time and once considered first also in merit,[1] the indirect responsibility for the shape and style of most of Dostoievsky's early work, and especially, through no fault of their own, for his limitations and mediocrity. It was only after he had freed himself from their influence that his own genius could fully emerge.

The influence of Gogol on Dostoievsky, as on all Russian literature of the generation, was simple and straightforward; that of Balzac was subtler and more profound. Gogol wrote a short story in 1842 called *The Cloak*, about a penurious clerk who saved up enough money to buy himself a new cloak, which was stolen from him on the first day he wore it, with the consequence that he died of a broken heart. This story had an astonishing success, which established the penurious clerk as a major figure in Russian literature. Hundreds of imitations and derivatives were written to echo the sentimental demonstration that " a man's a man for a' that." Among them were the majority of Dostoievsky's early works : the theme lies at the root of his first published book, *Poor Folk*, and at least four of the next half-dozen stories which followed it.

Balzac's deeper influence remained less easy to detect until after Dostoievsky had shaken it off. It is only in retrospect

[1] Nikolai Vasilievitch Gogol (1809–52) was a comic writer of great charm, chiefly famous for a rambling, incomplete novel called *Dead Souls* and a farcical play called *The Government Inspector*.

that the diametrical incompatibility of these two great geniuses can be seen. Compared in their maturity, the difference between the masterpieces of the two is almost a complete inversion. Balzac's approach to his characters was extrovert, Dostoievsky's introvert ; Balzac worked from the outside inwards, leaving character to emerge from incident ; Dostoievsky from the inside outwards, leaving incident to emerge from character. But Balzac's maturity was a generation earlier than Dostoievsky's ; and in his immaturity, Dostoievsky set about writing not his own novels but imitations first of Gogol and then of Balzac. He never succeeded with a novel of incident, and only found himself when he turned in the 1860's to the novel of character. By then he was in his forties, and the inordinate length of time he took to reach his maturity is the measure of the influences to which he succumbed. Even in his last works, he was still trying to achieve one aim which Balzac set before him in the work which first captured his imagination—the representation of a character of perfect saintliness. In this sense at least he never escaped from *Eugénie Grandet*, but fortunately this was a sense in which Balzac could do him no harm and only good.

Balzac's influence was slower to make itself felt on Dostoievsky than Gogol's, as well as slower to work itself out. *Poor Folk*, which was written in the winter of 1844–5 but not published until 1846, has Gogol writ large upon it, but the epistolary form in which it is written also owes something to the technique which Dostoievsky must have come across in English and French novelists of the eighteenth century. It consists of a series of letters between a penniless old clerk and a penniless young girl living nearby. He is in love with her, but she is unaware of it and regards him as a kindly old godfather. After many humiliations and hardships, she agrees to a disastrous marriage with an unpleasant admirer as the only escape from poverty, and the old clerk, still unable to declare his feelings, is naïvely called on for all manner of services and errands in connection with the wedding. The book is simple and moving : it would hardly support a tenth of Dostoievsky's reputation by itself, yet at the time it was held to be an astonishing masterpiece. One of the critics declared that " a new Gogol had appeared," thus unwittingly drawing attention to the least admirable fact about *Poor Folk*, that it had all been done before.

The story of its success has become legendary. Dostoievsky showed it to a young contemporary from the Military Engineering Academy, who read it through the night to the poet and critic, Nekrasov, who woke up Dostoievsky in the small hours to tell him that he had written a masterpiece. The verdict was confirmed by the great critic Byelinsky, whose word was canonical, and Dostoievsky's name was made in his literary circle. This circle already included the Maikov brothers, Valerian and Apollon, who were to become his closest friends, and the aristocratic writer, Turgenev, who was to become his bitterest rival. At first all alike combined to pet him. Dostoievsky was entranced by his reception, but he ruined it by his own *gaucherie*. All who knew him at that time agree that he was surly, suspicious and neurotic. Having wrongly assumed that he was now regarded as the greatest writer of the age, when he found that he was not he leapt to the equally wrong assumption that he was being mocked and insulted. The disillusionment was aggravated by his inability to write anything new as good as *Poor Folk*, as well as perhaps by an inconclusive flirtation with Nekrasov's mistress. Even while *Poor Folk* was appearing by instalments in Nekrasov's journal, *Almanach*,[1] Dostoievsky broke with

[1] Serialisation was the normal method of first publication at the time ; this accounts for the abrupt and often absurd divisions into chapters of most of Dostoievsky's novels, which were written in haste " to be continued in our next."

the circle and entered into a contract with a rival editor called Kraevsky, whom Byelinsky looked upon as " a grabber, a vampire and a cad." Many years later Dostoievsky resumed his friendship with Nekrasov, and he never lost contact with the Maikovs ; but with Turgenev he remained irreconcilable almost to the end, and Byelinsky died in 1848, too soon to see him redeem his follies.

That the circle was well rid of him for the time is evident from the short stories which followed *Poor Folk*, though no doubt their ineptitude was partly due to the entangling contract under which he found himself obliged to write to order for Kraevsky. His way out was simply to draw endlessly on Gogol's penurious clerk. *The Double* was about a clerk haunted and finally driven mad by his own *alter ego* ; *Mr. Prohartchin* was a clerk who disappeared from his lodgings, and reappeared, and died leaving an unexpected fortune in his mattress ; *Polzunkov* was a clerk who sent in his resignation as an April Fool, and was dumbfounded to find it accepted by his superior, who saw in it a way of escape from his own irregularities ; *A Faint Heart* was about a clerk who could not make up his mind to put his love before his copying work, and finally went mad and died out of sheer gratitude to the friend who did it for him. They are all of a dullness which might be thought unparalleled by anyone who had not read *The Landlady*, which achieves the rare distinction of being both dull and crazy, without even the merit which the others mostly have of being short. When Byelinsky read *The Landlady* (which is also known in English as *The Hostess* or *The Mistress of the House*), he described it as " abominable nonsense," adding that " every new work of Dostoievsky is a further step in his decline." It is difficult not to agree with him.

A salutary warning against attaching too much importance to the early works of great writers can be found in a recent attempt to make sense of *The Landlady*. The story relates the efforts of a young man to make the acquaintance of a girl living in a mysterious house under the protection of an old man who appears to be a criminal, a magician and a priest, related to her in a way that is not defined. Under the title of *The Mistress of the House*, a symbolic meaning has lately been found in it:[1] the young man represents the Russian intelligentsia, the girl is the Russian people, and the old man stands for the religious beliefs of the people, " above all for the schismatic Old Believers." This may be all very well for a symbol called the mistress of the house, but to English readers at least it seems incongruous for a landlady : such are the advantages of doing your own translation. The only substantial difference between this and the rest of Dostoievsky's drivel between 1846 and 1849 is that it seems not to be entirely derivative.

A few points of exception can be found to the general condemnation of Dostoievsky's work in this period as unreadable. One point is a real talent for humour, which English readers are not accustomed to expect in Russian writers, least of all in Dostoievsky. Pure humour is the whole substance of *Another Man's Wife*, which begins with a husband and a lover suspiciously fencing to determine whether the wife of the former and the mistress of the latter are in fact the same lady, and ends with both hiding under the bed of another lady, a stranger to both of them, while she tries to parry her own husband's suspicions. The same vein is apparent in *A Novel in Nine Letters* (though there are in fact eleven letters, and the point turns on the extra two) : the letters record an exasperated quarrel over a debt between two touchy friends, culminating in the simultaneous revelation by each to the other that each of their wives has been deceiving them simultaneously with the same third party, to whom the

[1] Mackiewicz, p. 34.

crucial two letters are addressed. This vein of humour is
not much noticed in Dostoievsky's work, though it is still
current in his most famous tragedies, as it is similarly in
Shakespeare's. It wore thinner in his later years, but he still
remained capable of filling a short story with it, as he did
later in *The Crocodile*, which tells how a respectable citizen
of Petersburg was swallowed by a crocodile on show in a
tank ; and how satisfactory and even commercially lucrative
he found his predicament, if only his wife and a friend or
two would come and join him.

But there is a more important reason why not all of
Dostoievsky's work immediately after *Poor Folk* can safely
be neglected. This is that many of his stories, though tiresome
in themselves, can be seen as preliminary sketches for parts
of his later masterpieces, presenting in a primitive form some
of the principal episodes and characters which were to occupy
his imagination throughout his creative life. One of the
recurrent themes is that of *The Double*, namely that no man's
character is simple and uniform, but all contain unresolved
contradictions. In *The Double* the point is clumsily made
by splitting the clerk into two physically identical twins, one
timid and ineffectual, the other masterful and hearty. This
technique works much less well than Stevenson's, which
never allowed Jekyll and Hyde to coexist at the same
moment and made them physically easy to distinguish.
Dostoievsky never hit upon Stevenson's technique, but he
was plainly dissatisfied with his own. Many years later
he planned to rewrite *The Double*,[1] but in the meantime he
tried next to depict straightforwardly a dual character in one
man : this effort he called *An Honest Thief*, the subject being
a man who could not help stealing but died of remorse at
having done so. The story is hardly more successful than

[1] This appears from his note-books, quoted in *Stavrogin's Confession, etc.*,
p. 150.

The Double, but it will serve as a pointer towards the triumphant solution of this problem which Dostoievsky achieved many years later.

There are three more of his favourite and most successful characters to be found adumbrated in his early stories. One is the romantic young lover who helps his beloved to find happiness with his rival out of sheer devotion : this character first appears as the hero of *White Nights*, and it is remarkable not only that the theme makes up the whole substance of this story as well as a main theme of many later works, but also that, in the years between, it became a role for which Dostoievsky cast himself in his own life.[1] The next of the recurrent characters is the lecherous old man attracted by an adolescent girl, which malicious biographers have mistaken for a self-portrait (despite the fact that Dostoievsky was intrigued by it as much in his twenties as in his fifties). This theme first appeared in *Poor Folk* ; two years later it made up the whole substance of *A Christmas Tree and a Wedding* ; and echoes of it are detectable in almost all his mature works. Finally the last of the recurrent characters to be first introduced in the early short stories is the adolescent child just becoming aware of approaching maturity : a girl in *Nyetochka Nyezvanov*, who tells her story in the first person, and a boy in *A Little Hero*, who wins the nickname by riding an unmanageable stallion which his adored heroine dare not mount. Both of these stories deserve to have a little more said of them, for several reasons : they rise above the mediocrity of his period 1846-9 ; they are technically interesting ; and most important of all, they were Dostoievsky's last works for ten years.

Nyetochka Nyezvanov, which was never completed, though a longer version was known to exist at the time,[2] is the story of a girl adopted from her father, an unsuccessful musician,

[1] See p. 33 below.   [2] See Soloviev, p. 120.

by a wealthy family as companion to their daughter, Katya.
The two girls fall in love with each other and are forcibly
separated. Nyetochka is removed to the care of Katya's
married elder sister, whose husband falls in love with her
while she is still a child. Other episodes in the book are
designed to show Nyetochka's physical and psychological
reaction to adolescence, but the story breaks off short of
becoming a full-length novel. It is a beautiful and moving
but ill-constructed piece of work, perhaps chiefly remarkable
for two reasons which have nothing to do with its merit.
One is that it so impressed a Petersburg family called Snitkin
that the nickname Nyetochka was given to their baby
daughter, Anna Grigoryevna, who was born in 1846 and
twenty years later became Dostoievsky's second wife. The
other reason is that *Nyetochka Nyezvanov* was Dostoievsky's
only attempt to tell a story in the first person through the
mouth of a feminine character, which makes its success at
least an unusual *tour de force*.

Narration in the first person was a practice which steadily
grew on Dostoievsky in his formative years, and one which
he never completely shook off. Of the fourteen stories so
far mentioned, six were told in the first person by an essential
participant, and two more in the first person through the
medium of letters. In his later works there is an even higher
proportion, and in most of the full-length novels of his
maturity a narrator in the first person is at least implied, or
was involved at some stage of the drafting, though in the
latest examples this narrator finally ceased to be an essential
participant in the story. The gradual intrusion of the narrator
as an essential participant in the earlier works, diminishing
in importance to a formal relic in the last, adds to the
plausibility of interpreting the earlier as sketches for the later :
each sketch being seen from one particular point of view—the
narrator's. For Dostoievsky was not yet able to enter

imaginatively into the full experience, amounting to self-identification, of more than one character at a time. This may perhaps be called a deficiency of his own experience.

It is not to be suggested that all fiction must necessarily be derived from the writer's experience, to the point of being merely autobiographical. But a man who has nothing to put into his autobiography has little to put into his novels either ; and this was true of Dostoievsky in a higher degree even than of most great writers. So far no experience of any extraordinary significance had befallen him (apart from his father's murder, to which his reaction was wholly sublimated), and his work reflected the deficiency as soon as he had exhausted the derivative potentialities of Gogol. But between the writing of *Nyetochka Nyezvanov* (1848) and the writing of *A Little Hero* (1849), which was to be his last work for a decade, the deficiency was remedied, abruptly, overwhelmingly, and all but tragically.

CHAPTER II

FAILURE

THE value of Byelinsky's circle to Dostoievsky had been that it offered him a firm base not only in literature but also in society. When he cut himself off from it in a tantrum, he chose a very much worse literary base in the clutches of his new editor, Kraevsky ; but even this was harmless enough compared to his choice of a new social base, which was disastrous. Probably through his friends, the Maikov brothers, Dostoievsky was introduced to a romantically conspiratorial official in the Ministry of Foreign Affairs, called Petrashevsky, who had formed round himself a circle of what to-day we might call " parlour pinks." No better description of the aimless futility of this circle could be given than Dostoievsky's own satire twenty years later : [1]

> . . . it was asserted that at the time there was discovered in Petersburg a vast, unnatural and illegal conspiracy of thirty people which almost shook society to its foundations. It was said that they were positively on the point of translating Fourier.

Fourier was a mad French socialist, who held that society should be organised in " phalanxes " of 1600 each, living in what he called " phalansteries " ; and it is undeniably true that Petrashevsky's circle celebrated his birthday with a banquet. Dostoievsky was joined in this adventure by his brother Mihail, and also unfortunately by a police-spy. He

[1] *The Possessed*, p. 3.

went so far as to read to Petrashevsky's circle a famous letter
written by Byelinsky to Gogol, attacking him for his con-
version to religious and political orthodoxy. He even went
further : after many months had proved that Petrashevsky's
circle was going the way of all circles, Dostoievsky joined a
smaller and bolder group led by another civil servant called
Durov, who actually contemplated the establishment of an
illegal printing-press.

If Petrashevsky went about as far as the Fabians, Durov's
circle was at least as dangerous as the I.L.P. ; and the Tsarist
police, having failed to penetrate the smaller circle, as they
had the larger, decided to take no risks. 1848 had been the
year of Europe's revolutions and the Communist Manifesto.
1849 was the year of reaction : on the night of 22–23 April
thirty-four supposed members of Petrashevsky's circle were
arrested, including Dostoievsky and even (by mistake) his
brother Andrey, who was not a member. A fortnight later
Mihail was arrested in place of Andrey, who was released,
and four months later Mihail was released among others for
lack of evidence. Possibly Dostoievsky himself had no real
sense of danger, for he passed his time in prison writing
A Little Hero, one of the calmest and most charming short
stories of his first period, as well as the last ; and it betrays
not an inkling of foreboding. But on 16 November he was
found guilty of revolutionary conspiracy.

The trial was a farce ; the sequel was a gruesome mockery
of justice. A military court recommended sentence of death
for twenty-one out of twenty-three accused, including
Dostoievsky ; and although the Tsar commuted the sentences,
it was decided to make an example of them by bringing them
out before a firing-squad. The cruel pretence, which took
place on 22 December 1849, was interrupted at the last
moment by the well-timed entry of a messenger carrying the
order of reprieve ; the prisoners were taken back to gaol

to await removal to Siberia and elsewhere. One of them had already gone mad from the experience. It is fortunate that this turning-point in Dostoievsky's life is commemorated by a letter to Mihail written a few hours later on the same day.[1] It may be counted the first cry of his rebirth, and it is even more impressive, because instant and unconsidered, than the many passages in his later works which revert to the hideous torture of that day.[2]

Dostoievsky's sentence, like Durov's, was to penal servitude for eight years, which the Tsar altered in his own hand to " four years and then to serve as a common soldier." In the early hours of Christmas Day, 1849, they set out for Siberia, a journey of several weeks by sleigh. They halted on the way for six days at Tobolsk, where they were visited by the wives of some of the survivors from the " Decabrist plot " of 1825. One of them gave Dostoievsky a Bible, which remained with him for the rest of his life. Three days later they reached the convict-prison at Omsk, and Dostoievsky passed into what he himself called " the house of the dead."

It is impossible to follow him there except through the pages of the book which he wrote under that name many years later, a book which it is impossible to describe or summarise. Everyone has his own idea of what Siberia means : it is enough that it should stand for the worst extreme of suffering that can be imagined. Yet in this century we have learned that it is not the worst.[3] On the assumption that Siberia under the Communists is little changed from Tsarist days, we can see that it differed and still differs from the Nazi concentration camp in the almost total absence

[1] See Koteliansky, pp. 5 *seqq.*
[2] See especially *The Idiot*, pp. 59 *seqq.*
[3] It even reminded Maurice Baring in some respects of Eton : see *Landmarks in Russian Literature*, p. 171.

of purely deliberate cruelty.[1] The only officer in Dostoievsky's time who committed deliberate cruelty on the prisoners was removed and degraded. The first portraits of Dostoievsky after his condemnation (taken in 1858 and 1863) show no sign of suffering. He seems, from his own account compared with that of a Polish fellow-prisoner, to have suffered most from his unpopularity with his companions, which may well have rested largely on the importance he attached to his own "nobility." He hated the Poles, and never spoke to Durov in prison. It is difficult to tell how much he suffered from the appalling conditions of life at Omsk, because in the mellow retrospect of later years [2] he was at pains to write with a dispassionate and almost mystical detachment and in the guise of fiction.[3] He claimed to have recovered from some of his nervous ailments in Siberia, but probably it was also at this time that he began to have epileptic fits, from which he was never again free. It is at least hard to doubt, however, that without the experience of Siberia he would never have written the masterpieces of his later years.

The gap of four years after 1849 in Dostoievsky's biography can only be bridged by reading *The House of the Dead*. There can be no substitute for it ; and thanks to it, a biographical leap forward in time can be made to 15 February 1854, when he was released from prison to serve another five years as a common soldier. He was posted to the 7th Infantry Battalion at Semipalatinsk, in what is now called Kazakhstan, a southern province of the U.S.S.R. It lay on the fringe of the world of the *Arabian Nights*, but the association meant nothing to

[1] Cp., *e.g.*, *The Dark Side of the Moon* (by an anonymous Polish woman) with *Day After Day* (by Odd Nansen) for Siberian and Nazi concentration camps in the 1940's.

[2] *The House of the Dead* was published in 1861.

[3] He represents the imaginary narrator as a murderer, though it is obviously himself : this is a characteristic piece of snobbery, like that of a penitent claiming to be the worst of all sinners.

Dostoievsky, whose life there was a drab and colourless routine of drudgery. The only relief was the arrival in November 1854 of the new District Prosecutor, an excellent young man called Baron Wrangel, to whom Dostoievsky owed more than he could ever acknowledge or repay. In later years Wrangel often helped him with money ; but his first service was to contribute to his moral and social rehabilitation. He received Dostoievsky in his house and introduced him to the local governor—both breaches of etiquette while Dostoievsky remained a private soldier. He also connived at Dostoievsky's first known love-affair, with the wife of a minor official called Alexander Isayev, who already had a small son, Pavel (Pasha) by name, an unpleasant child destined to become more so.

Wrangel himself described Maria Dmitrievna Isayev as " a rather pretty blonde of middle height, very thin, passionate and *exaltée* " ; she was also consumptive. He obviously disapproved of the connection as unworthy of Dostoievsky, but his kind heart carried him into many irregularities. When Isayev was transferred to another post in 1855, Wrangel contrived to enable Dostoievsky to accompany the family on part of the way, the Baron and Isayev and the child in one carriage followed by Dostoievsky and Maria Isayev in a cart. For a year the lovers continued to correspond ; but a meeting which Wrangel planned for them did not take place, because Maria found herself unable to leave her husband on his sick-bed. It was his last illness, the consequence of years of alcoholism : he died in August 1856, and Dostoievsky immediately began to plan marriage with the widow. His own position was already much improved, since he had been twice promoted in 1856, first to N.C.O. and then to commissioned rank ; and more important still, the death of Tsar Nicholas I in 1855 had been followed by immediate tokens of official liberalisation, which included an amnesty for the Petrashevsky group, and the removal of the ban, imposed automatically by the official censorship in 1849, on the publication of Dostoievsky's writings.[1]

Maria was of a type suited to his artistic temperament, if not to his passionate heart. She kept him on tenterhooks for many months, and even after she had agreed to marry him, it is said that she continued to give her favours to another rival. Dostoievsky knew of this, and offered his services as a go-between, faithfully basing himself on the hero of his own *White Nights*, who was to grow into so many characters in his mature masterpieces. Maria probably regarded the marriage solely as one of convenience ; and even the convenience must have seemed doubtful a few days after the wedding (which took place on 6 February 1857), when she learned for the first time by bitter experience that she was the wife of an epileptic. Yet Dostoievsky was able to tell Wrangel many years later that

> " . . . although we were decidedly unhappy together, owing to her strange, suspicious and morbidly imaginative character, we could not cease to love one another ; the more unhappy we were, the more we became attached to each other."

This certainly rings true of Dostoievsky himself, and it is perhaps unlikely that his customary penetration of another's feelings failed him in the case of his wife.

Fortunately his material position continued to improve, no doubt largely thanks to Wrangel's efforts. A curiously servile petition to the new Tsar, Alexander II,[2] eventually

[1] The censor from 1856–60 was Goncharov, author of the enchanting novel *Oblomov*, which established the legendary type of the amiable, ineffectual Russian.

[2] Dostoievsky never blamed the Tsar for his unjust sufferings : he shared the conventional view expressed in the Russian proverb : " Oppression comes not from the Tsar but from his favourites."

secured for him permission to resign his commission in 1858
and to return to Russia in 1859. At first he was allowed only
to settle at Tver, between Moscow and Petersburg; but four
months later he was allowed to go to Moscow, where he
arrived with Maria and his stepson Pasha in December 1859. He
was at last free to resume unhampered his literary career, which
had been defunct since 1849 and commemorated in the meantime only by the posthumous publication of *A Little Hero* in 1857.

The first-fruits of his new life were unpromising. He
published two short novels called *Uncle's Dream* and *The
Friend of the Family*, and collaborated with his brother Mihail
in founding a journal called *Vremya*, which first came out in
January 1861. The two novels were failures, and *Vremya's*
success was short-lived. *Uncle's Dream* is a tedious story of
a vain old millionaire whom a scheming mother induces to
propose to her daughter: a scheme which is frustrated by a
rival for the daughter's love, who convinces the old man
that he dreamed the whole episode. It is only interesting as
an intermediate development of Dostoievsky's sexual theme
linking the elderly *roué* with the adolescent girl; it is a
reprint from the past turned into a sketch for the future.[1]
The Friend of the Family is the story of a domestic parasite
who makes himself alike intolerable and indispensable to a
wealthy provincial household, with the result that when he
and the head of the house eventually decide upon a final
breach, both discover that it is impossible as soon as they put
it into effect. The idea is original and interesting, but clumsily
worked out in this first attempt on it. The suggestion has
been made that *The Friend of the Family* is a literary satire
on Byelinsky,[2] though Kraevsky (who was again Dostoievsky's

[1] The theme takes its final form, closely modelled on *Uncle's Dream*,
in *A Raw Youth* (1875).

[2] Mackiewicz, p. 77: he calls the book *The Hamlet of Stepanchikovo*,
which corresponds to the Russian title.

publisher in this case) is said to have identified the parasite
with Gogol. Both notions seem ludicrously off the point,
but if there is anything in either of them, it only shows how
out of touch Dostoievsky was with the changed world to
which he had returned.

This was hardly surprising, for the intervening decade had
brought great changes to Russia. Not only had Byelinsky
been dead more than ten years, and Gogol five, but political
conditions were altogether different. Industrialisation was at
last under way, bringing capitalism with it. The death of
Nicholas I in 1855 had been followed by an attempt at
Liberalism under his successor, Alexander II ; the Crimean
War (1854–56) had shaken Russian complacency and induced
a mood of nationalism and revenge ; the opening of the
Berlin-Petersburg railway had renewed the connection
between Russia and Western Europe, which precipitated
itself among Russian intellectuals in the form of an endless
quarrel between Slavophils and Westerners, those who
shunned and those who sought inspiration from the West. All
these things played their part in Dostoievsky's later works :
he came to satirise the liberalism of the 1850's, to applaud
the nationalism of Holy Russia, and to reconcile momentarily
the deep differences of Slavophil and Western sentiment. But
there is little trace of any of these things in the first works
after his return from Siberia.

Indirectly this disharmony with the spirit of the times
accounted for the eventual demise of his new journal, *Vremya*.
The men who helped him found it, including his old friend
Apollon Maikov and a new friend, Strakhov (who later
became his biographer), called themselves " men of the soil,"
meaning the native soil of Russia ; in other words, they
were Slavophils, but they had not clearly thought out the
implications. In Dostoievsky's literary biography this venture,
although for two years relatively successful, was also relatively

unimportant. A few scanty items sum it up. The first and most important was the serialisation of *The House of the Dead*, which made a considerable impression, in 1861 ; the second was the serialisation in the same year of his first long work of fiction since *Poor Folk*, a melodramatic imitation of Dickens and Balzac called *The Insulted and Injured* ; the third was his last essay on the theme of Gogol's clerk, a short story called *An Unpleasant Predicament* ; the fourth, of a different order, was the publication in September 1861 of a short story by a girl called Apollinaria Suslova, who became as an eventual result Dostoievsky's mistress. The financial success of *Vremya*, which was certainly due to Dostoievsky rather than his fellow-contributors, enabled him to make his first journey abroad in 1862 : he visited Germany, France, Switzerland, Italy and England (where he met the famous revolutionary Herzen, who was living in exile like most famous revolutionaries of the day) ; and on his return he wrote a book about the trip, like any good tourist, called *Winter Notes on Summer Impressions*.

In fact Dostoievsky was in danger of finding straight journalism a more satisfactory profession than writing fiction. *The House of the Dead* was what we should call a " documentary " rather than a novel, and both *The Insulted and Injured* and *An Unpleasant Predicament* were wholly unoriginal. The last is simply the old story of the penurious clerk seen, by way of a change, from the point of view of his official superior, who attends the clerk's wedding-feast uninvited, on an impulse of liberal benevolence and pompous magnanimity, and after ruining the party for everyone, finishes the night in a drunken stupor on the nuptial bed. *The Insulted and Injured* is a hotch-potch made up of the pathetic little orphan borrowed from Dickens, the self-sacrificing lover from *White Nights*, and the nasty old man from several of Dostoievsky's early works : the result is a straightforward novel of incident in the manner of Balzac, which would serve the newcomer to Dostoievsky as a very easy but somewhat misleading introduction. It is questionable how long this sort of thing would have kept *Vremya* going, if disaster had not fallen on it in 1863 through Dostoievsky's political innocence.

The trouble came from Poland. Even those Russians who called themselves Slavophils found it hard to extend their Liberalism to the Poles, whose ancestors (though Slavs) had committed the blunder of becoming Roman Catholics instead of Orthodox Christians. When the Poles found that Alexander II's Liberal measures (which had liberated the serfs in 1861 and given a degree of autonomy to the universities in 1863) scarcely penetrated within the frontiers of historical Poland, they rose in revolt. Such an event had last happened in 1830–31, when Dostoievsky was a child, and in 1863 it took the Liberals by surprise. There was no difficulty about suppressing the revolt, but no honest intellectual knew what to say about it without betraying either his patriotic beliefs or his Liberalism. *Vremya* ignored it for some time, but finally published an obscure article (not by Dostoievsky but by Strakhov) called *A Fatal Question*, which intended to support the Tsarist government but was regarded as attacking it : a mistake that may be accounted typical of the Russian censorship, which at that time banned both Hobbes and Spinoza but admitted Marx. *Vremya* was suppressed, and Dostoievsky was obliged to borrow money (from the Fund for Assisting Needy Men of Letters) for his second journey abroad in 1863.

His wife had long been seriously ill, and there was no question of her ever accompanying him. He was accompanied instead by Apollinaria Suslova ; or rather, he made desparate efforts to accompany her, for she deliberately tortured him with capricious alternations of provocation and denial. They travelled to Paris (he pursuing her), to Germany, Switzerland and Italy (as " brother and sister," at her imperious demand), and back *via* Germany, where she left him. It is not surprising that under the strain of this ambiguous liaison, Dostoievsky first succumbed to the perilous attractions of roulette at Wiesbaden. He saw Polina, as he called his unaccommodating mistress, only intermittently for the rest of his life, though he continued to correspond with her not only during the rest of his first marriage but in the early years of his second. There is no doubt that he learned much about sexual psychology from her, as his writings in the next few years attest ; but there were two more unfortunate legacies of this abortive adventure. One was a passion for gambling, which played havoc with his irregular finances for nearly ten years ; the other was a still more bitter recrudescence of his quarrel with Turgenev, who had abandoned Russia and settled in Baden, where Dostoievsky visited him in August 1863. The two misfortunes were connected, for Dostoievsky borrowed money from Turgenev, which he was never able to repay, to cover the inadequacies of his " system " at the roulette table.

In October 1863 he returned in a desperate state of mind to Petersburg, where he was joined by his wife and stepson from Moscow. With the help of a legacy from his uncle Kumanin, who had died in that year, he was able to start a new journal, the *Epokha*, in place of the *Vremya* ; and in it he published the last and most significant work of these years of unsettled confusion, the *Letters from the Underworld*. The book is remarkable not for its form, which is a perfectly pointless division into two unrelated halves, one a rambling monograph and the other a rambling short story, but for the emergence through this chaotic presentation of a new idea, which may be called the anatomy of irrational malice, of the instinct to choose evil deliberately in preference to good : Shakespeare's Iago is the ancestral prototype. Because the idea is worked out in the total isolation which the narrator of *Letters from the Underworld* imposes on his life, as it were in laboratory conditions, the effect is unconvincing, for conscious wickedness can only seem significant, as Shakespeare made it, against a background of normality ; but the book is interesting as a prefigurement of some of Dostoievsky's most astonishing characters to come, and it is an eloquent testimony to the spiritual torment of his relationship with Apollinaria Suslova.

The momentary success which *Letters from the Underworld* helped to bring to the *Epokha* was soon swallowed up in a succession of misfortunes which overwhelmed Dostoievsky for more than two years. In April 1864 his wife died, leaving him with the responsibility for her wastrel son, Pasha. In July 1864 his brother Mihail died, leaving a mountain of debts and a penniless widow and children ; and this responsibility too Dostoievsky took upon himself, though there was no obligation to do so. Desperate for money, he tried everything except writing : it was not until January 1866, when the first instalment of *Crime and Punishment* appeared, that he earned another penny with his pen, and then it was not in the *Epokha*, which had already foundered, but in the Moscow journal, *Russky Vestnik*, edited by Katkov, who became an unfailing friend in need. Dostoievsky had struggled unsuccessfully to keep alive the *Epokha* (of which nominally he was not even the editor) in order to pay off his brother's debts, but the last number came out in February 1865. He tried to borrow money wherever he could find it : from Katkov before a line of *Crime and Punishment* was delivered ; from Herzen, whom he had met again in Italy ; from any of his fellow-journalists who happened to be in funds ; and above all from Baron Wrangel, whom he found in Copenhagen during a third journey abroad in 1865. But the most desperate step of all was to commit himself to a lunatic contract with an unscrupulous publisher called Stellovsky, to whom he promised, in return for an advance of 3000 roubles, a full-length novel by November 1866, with the penalty of ceding to him the copyright of all his books, past or future, if he failed to deliver it in time.

There was nothing particularly difficult about the fulfilment of the contract when it was signed in 1865. Dostoievsky therefore forgot all about it until it was almost too late. The intervening year was filled with sentimental distractions, apart from desultory work on *Crime and Punishment* for Katkov. He had a final brush with Apollinaria Suslova, a briefly satisfactory affair with an adventuress called Martha (who had acquired by marriage the surname of Brown), and a flirtation, which was perhaps not far from becoming a marriage, with a brilliant and charming young girl called Anna Korvin-Krukovskaya, who entered his life ironically by the same route as Polina, as a contributor to the *Epokha*. There was nothing remarkable about the part played in Dostoievsky's life by any of these passing attractions, except that each of them provided him with different aspects of the most successful feminine characters in his mature works. But their passage helped to make the prospect of fulfilling Stellovsky's contract increasingly hopeless. By September 1866 he had not yet written a line of the novel which had to be delivered by the beginning of November. Maikov and other friends offered to help him by writing parts of it for him, but Dostoievsky refused. At the last moment, when all seemed lost, inspiration suggested another solution, which turned out to be the second great turning-point in his life, no less crucial and revolutionary than the first : but this time it was the happy ending.

CHAPTER III

REDEMPTION

IT was suggested to Dostoievsky that the way out of his
danger from Stellovsky was to dictate the required novel
to a stenographer. He applied for one from a training-
school, and was sent Anna Grigoryevna Snitkin, who eighteen
years before had been nicknamed Nyetochka from his early
novel. It is curious that a Russian girl in the 1860's could
go freely to take dictation from an unknown. man, which
she certainly could not at the time in England or America.
It is ironical as well as curious that the story which Dostoievsky
began to dictate to her on 4 October 1866, under the title
of The Gambler, was an unblushing and more or less straightforward account of his complex relations with Polina Suslova.
It is the most directly autobiographical of his novels, even
to the point of including a clear portrait of his wealthy aunt
Kumanina, his mother's sister and Kumanin's widow, whose
death and fortune were eagerly awaited by the entire family :
it is almost as if he were giving his stenographer a preview of
life among the Dostoievskys. The outcome of it was that
he not only cheated Stellovsky of his pound of flesh, but
acquired a new and perfect wife.

Her first entry into his life, and the months which followed
it, are narrated in great detail in the reminiscences which
Anna put together in her old age, from shorthand notes taken
at the time, and from the diary which she kept for several
months in 1867. Though she was no genius, and in fact her
whole value to Dostoievsky lay in the placid ordinariness of
her temperament, nevertheless it is a just tribute to her quality
to say that there can no more be offered any substitute for

her diary and reminiscences during this period of Dostoievsky's biography, than there can for *The House of the Dead* during the Siberian period. They deserve to be read in their own right, as an incomparable account of the trials of life with a genius ; and what is more, only from them will the reader become aware (though Anna was perhaps unaware) how much she contributed to the final flowering of that genius. Her entry into his life was the antithesis to which the disaster of 1849 was the thesis ; and the synthesis was a decade and a half of unparalleled creation.

The first-fruits of Dostoievsky's collaboration with Anna were the completion of *The Gambler* on 30 October, a proposal of marriage on 8 November, the completion of *Crime and Punishment* by the end of the year, and a wedding on 15 February 1867. It is not surprising that *Crime and Punishment* (the first and perhaps the most famous, but certainly the least substantial, of Dostoievsky's great masterpieces) shows distinct signs of the whirlwind courtship in its closing pages. It is a good example of the invariable and inevitable method of his work, which was never planned exhaustively in advance, but rushed to the press, instalment by instalment, with consequent inconsistencies of detail and fluctuations of mood that the serial method of publication never enabled him to rectify. In this respect he was always sorrowfully contrasting himself with Turgenev, the wealthy aristocrat who wrote as he liked, and Anna herself recorded that : [1]

> Never in all his life (except when he wrote *Poor Folk*) was Fyodor Mihailovitch able to write anything at his leisure, without needing to hurry or to think out the details of a novel and thoroughly to reason out the plan—in short *create* a work.

Crime and Punishment, being his longest novel yet, was a good example of what she meant. It cannot be called totally

[1] See Hill and Mudie, pp. 366–8 (note 178).

unplanned, because a first project for it was offered to his former publisher Kraevsky in 1865 under the title of *The Tipplers*, and at one stage the story was to have been told in the first person, as *The Friend of the Family* and *The Gambler* had been. But there were still more structural changes to come even after the first instalments had been published.

Crime and Punishment is the story of a poor student, Rodion Raskolnikov, and a poor girl, Sonia Marmeladov, the daughter of a drunken father and a consumptive mother, reputed to be based on Isayev and Dostoievsky's first wife Maria. The setting is Petersburg, which is henceforth always the urban background, in preference to Moscow, of all the novels. Before Sonia and Raskolnikov meet, she has become a prostitute as the only means of supporting her family, and he a murderer, not only of his intended victim, an old woman money-lender, but also, for self-protection, of her imbecile sister, who caught him in the act. Sonia's motive was at least simple, but Raskolnikov's motive confused three separate impulses, which may be distinguished as the moral, the immoral and the amoral. The moral motive was that the old woman was an evil creature who deserved ·to die, and whose death would benefit many and harm none. The immoral motive was that Raskolnikov needed money, principally to save his sister Dounia from a disastrous marriage : Dounia had already been the victim of advances from her unpleasant employer, Svidrigailov, and had then in despair agreed to marry a scarcely less unpleasant individual called Luzhin. The amoral motive was Raskolnikov's conviction that he belonged, like Napoleon, to a class of supermen for whom " all things are lawful "—a theme which he had rashly developed in a published article.

Raskolnikov's inability to clarify his own motives is the cause of his downfall : experience teaches him that he is not a superman, and the second murder destroys his moral

case. The remainder of the book is occupied by a struggle
for his fate between three people : Sonia, to whom he confesses the murder ; Svidrigailov, who overhears the confession ; and a psychologically cunning detective, who
suspects him from his behaviour but can find no proof. The
most interesting of the three is Svidrigailov, who first enters
the book as an afterthought exactly half-way through. He
is unmistakably Raskolnikov's *alter ego*, the embodiment of
the evil motives which Dostoievsky could not after all combine
in one character with the mere weakness of Raskolnikov.
Svidrigailov is in fact a redraft both of *The Double* and of
the narrator of *Letters from the Underworld*. He completely
understands the immoral motive of Raskolnikov's murders,
just as the detective understands the amoral motive of the
would-be superman. But in the end the victory is Sonia's :
she persuades Raskolnikov to confess, and accompanies him
to Siberia ; the detective attributes it all to his own cunning,
and Svidrigailov commits a macabre suicide. The somewhat
abrupt and novelettish ending can reasonably be attributed
to Dostoievsky's preoccupation with more agreeable ideas
in the last two months of 1866.

When *Crime and Punishment* was finished and the marriage
celebrated, Anna proved her mettle at once by carrying
Dostoievsky off abroad. This was partly to escape his debts,
which even the success of *Crime and Punishment* did not go
far to cover, but chiefly to escape his relations, who treated
Dostoievsky as a milch-cow and Anna as a scheming
adventuress. The vilest of her enemies was Dostoievsky's
stepson Pasha, who openly proclaimed his intention to live
at his stepfather's expense and insulted Anna whenever they
met ; but not far behind him was Mihail's widow, who took
advantage of Dostoievsky's absence abroad to appropriate
his furniture, leaving Pasha to sell his library. One of the
most admirable traits in Dostoievsky's character was the

generosity with which he defended his worthless relations against Anna's justified criticisms, without at the same time losing her love. It was perhaps easier to do this during the four years from 1867 to 1871, which he passed entirely abroad from Russia and out of their clutches.

The four years of exile were not altogether pleasant for Dostoievsky, but for Anna they were often a nightmare. Only four months after leaving Petersburg, Dostoievsky wrote to Maikov in August 1867 : [1]

> I need Russia, I need her for my writing and for my work (without mentioning the rest of life), and how badly I need her.

It might be thought that he could have found sufficient consolation for his homesickness in his charming young wife, but in these early days of remarriage he was equally afraid of boring her and being bored by her across the gap of twenty-five years which separated their ages. Unfortunately for Anna he sought consolation instead in roulette, for which he had found out the infallible system of " simply keeping calm." Anna may have doubted whether it would work, but Dostoievsky never even gave it a chance : he lost his head and his money almost unfailingly at every visit to the tables. The story of their fantastic trek through Germany, Switzerland, Italy and Austria, in search of peace for Anna and a fortune for Dostoievsky, emerges vividly not only from Anna's diary and reminiscences, but also surprisingly from Dostoievsky's letters to her, which are as numerous in the first year of their marriage as at almost any other time.

[1] Anna, p. 203. It was Turgenev's preference for life in Western Europe, coupled with Dostoievsky's inability to repay what he owed him, that reopened the quarrel between them when they met in Baden in July 1867 : Dostoievsky advised Turgenev to buy a telescope to see what Russia was like before writing about it again.

The reason was that Anna was usually left elsewhere during his gambling expeditions, partly because she feared to distract him, partly because the hotel bills could seldom be discharged to enable her to move, and partly because of her successive pregnancies.

Her courage was boundless. She bore him two daughters abroad, one of whom (Sonia) died at three months in May 1868, and the other (Aimée) lived to write a somewhat unreliable biography of her father half a century later. (The rest of their family, two boys, came later in less uncomfortable circumstances : Fyodor in July 1871, and Alyosha, who died in infancy, in August 1875.) Dostoievsky was terribly affected by Sonia's death, and wrote in a revealing letter to Maikov, who was her godfather, begging him not to let Pasha and other members of the family know about his loss, for fear of their want of sympathy.[1] Apart from the burden and sorrow of making a family life in foreign towns, Anna had to put up with the erratic temperament and periodic epilepsy of her husband, and with the chronic destitution to which his habits reduced them. Yet to her honour she not only never faltered in her conviction of his genius, but actually encouraged his gambling expeditions as the only means of eliminating the virus from his system. At Dresden, for instance, in May 1867, when he left her on a disastrous trip to Homburg, she wrote in her diary :

> To go there is his dream. It is absolutely essential that he should go, or the thought of it will give him no peace. I am glad to think he will have his amusement, and come back to me as the loving person he used to be, although I cannot complain of his lack of love now either. He promises me that if he wins I am to go there too, and we shall live happily together. That would be nice—but after all I don't know— perhaps it would be better not to go at all.

[1] Carr, p. 179.

The whole strength and weakness of her feminine temperament, perfectly complementary to his own, are revealed in
that quotation. Equally revealing are the inevitable conse-
quences seen in his letters from Homburg, which admit the
loss of every penny and ask her to send more (by pawning
her possessions) through a banker's order, culminating in an
agonised appeal not to send it to Hamburg by mistake.[1]

On the rare occasions when he won, every kind of
extravagant luxury was lavished on Anna ; but she contrived
occasionally to save a little for mere necessities. She was
able to record in July 1867 : [2]

> . . . it is very pleasant to have those forty-four *louis* in
> our pockets, if even only for a short time. It's so much better
> than to have only two *louis* and to be uncertain as to what is
> going to happen next.

She was indeed right. The short time turned out to be less
than twenty-four hours, and the process was repeated with
devastating regularity for the next three years : at one time
they were so destitute that, having already pawned all Anna's
trinkets, Dostoievsky complained in a letter that he could not
tell the time because he had even pawned his own watch.
It seems almost miraculous that occasionally he was persuaded
to try to make a living by his pen instead of a fortune by his
system. Nevertheless, he completed two novels while he
was abroad, and began another ; and of the three, though
one was relatively unimportant, the other two belong to
the very front rank of his achievement.

The first of the two completed abroad, mainly in 1868, is
called *The Idiot*. It is the story of the brief sojourn in Russia
of Prince Myshkin, the last of an aristocratic family, who
arrives there from a mental home in Switzerland and returns
to it a few months later. He is an attractive young man, but

[1] Hill and Mudie, p. 14.   [2] Anna, p. 81.

an epileptic, looked upon by everyone, including himself, as abnormal ; and Dostoievsky intended to represent him not only as a saint but even as a reincarnation of Christ. The people whose lives his path crosses fall into four main groups, which are also themselves interlinked. There is first the family of the wealthy General Epanchin, a distant relative of Myshkin : he has a feather-brained wife and three lovely daughters, of whom the youngest, Aglaia, carries traces of Dostoievsky's brief attraction to Anna Korvin-Krukovskaya. Secondly there is the household of the impoverished General Ivolgin, where Myshkin lodges in Petersburg : this includes a daughter, Varvara, and two sons, Gavril (General Epanchin's business secretary) and Kolya (a schoolboy of thirteen). The third group, centred on a drunken buffoon called Lebedyev, includes a comic gang of would-be nihilists and roughs, as well as the pathetic figures of Lebedyev's motherless daughter Vera, who falls quietly in love with Myshkin, and a dying boy called Ippolit, who fails ludicrously in a pitiful attempt at suicide. The fourth and last group consists simply of two tremendous figures : the courtesan Nastasya, who carries traces of Dostoievsky's affair with Martha Brown, and her lover Rogozhin, whose hypnotic personality has its origins in the weird magician of *The Landlady*. The point of all this strangely assorted galaxy is to show how the saintly influence of Myshkin affects the most diverse types : calming the brilliant, neurotic Aglaia and the embittered youth Ippolit ; restoring the self-respect of the down-at-heel General Ivolgin and the notorious courtesan Nastasya ; winning the affection of his would-be enemies Gavril, Lebedyev and the nihilists ; and finally attaining an inconceivable harmony with his demonic antitype, Rogozhin —the wolf dwelling with the lamb.

Yet this is only one of the things *The Idiot* is about, and in a conventional sense it is not a novel about anything at all. The narrative simply proceeds, with Prince Myshkin, from group to group in a series of long and fascinating dialogues, which brilliantly establish character and continuity, but almost nothing else. The single thread of plot is spun out of Myshkin's own inner conflict—his simultaneous love for Aglaia and Nastasya.[1] After alternating again and again between the two, after nearly marrying Aglaia and nearly being murdered by Nastasya's lover Rogozhin, Prince Myshkin reaches the climax of his agony in one of the most moving and marvellous scenes of all literature : a night of vigil with Rogozhin beside the murdered corpse of Nastasya, from which they both emerge insane. In the morning : [2]

> . . . they found the murderer completely unconscious and raving. Myshkin was sitting beside him motionless on the floor, and every time the delirious man broke into screaming or babble, he hastened to pass his trembling hand softly over his hair and cheeks, as though caressing and soothing him.

Yet even that is not what *The Idiot* is about ; and perhaps it is no more possible to describe what it is about than a Beethoven symphony. There is only one thing to do with such a book : to read it, and re-read it, and re-read it again and again.

The Idiot was serialised by Katkov in the *Russky Vestnik*, as *Crime and Punishment* had been before it. Dostoievsky was heavily indebted to Katkov, who was not ungenerous with advances ; but this did not prevent him from picking up

---

[1] Dostoievsky had already touched on the possibility of a man loving two women equally at once in *The Insulted and Injured*, where it was completely unconvincing : the contrast of his success in *The Idiot* is in part the measure of his own experience in the meantime, when Anna Korvin-Krukovskaya and Martha Brown filled his life simultaneously See p. 40 above.

[2] *The Idiot*, p. 601.

what money he could find elsewhere. With a tactlessness which would have been called unscrupulous in a more business-like man, Dostoievsky obtained an advance at the same time from a rival editor for another novel not yet written. To fulfil the bargain, he dashed off a lightweight piece in three months of 1869, under the title of *The Eternal Husband*. The theme of it is that the eternal triangle presupposes not only a typical seducer but a typical cuckold, the two being logically inseparable as hill and valley, and indispensable to each other like the parasite and his host in *The Friend of the Family*. The "eternal husband" learns only after his wife's death that she had a series of lovers, and that her child is not his : he sets out to find the child's father, settles in his house, nearly murders him, abandons the child, plans a new marriage with an adolescent girl, but always finds himself unable to leave the rival who cheated him. From the barest outline, the book is obviously a hotch-potch of old themes : the unhappy orphan from *The Insulted and Injured*, the inseparable enemies from *The Double* and *The Idiot*, the sexual attraction of adolescence for middle age from *A Christmas Tree and a Wedding*, *Nyetochka Nyezvanov*, *Uncle's Dream* and many others. But more important is the new theme, still to be fully developed in later works, that only the thickness of a razor's edge separates love from hate.[1] This would have served to make the story into the basis of at least a minor reputation, but in Dostoievsky's career it can only be counted a pot-boiling trifle.

Its publication in 1870 in a rival journal constituted a breach of etiquette if not of contract towards Katkov. Dostoievsky had a moral obligation to write something for him to repay his advances, and to write it soon. Already

---

[1] Cp. *The Brothers Karamazov*, p. 731, Dmitri to Katerina : " We've hated each other for many things, Katya, but I swear, I swear I loved you even while I hated you, and you didn't love me ! "

before *The Idiot* was finished, Dostoievsky had formed a project for a colossal novel, or a series of novels, to be known as *The Life of a Great Sinner*. This was never written, but the copious notes made for it in his note-books were drawn upon for all the three major novels which he was still to write. The first of them, which was begun in 1870, is usually known in English as *The Possessed*, or sometimes as *The Devils*; but it might more usefully be called *The Gadarene Swine*, for that is the symbolism of the story.[1] The swine into whom the devils enter are a group of revolutionaries under the influence of a megalomaniac; and since the theme comprises not only the potentialities of revolution but also the abuse of power, it is perhaps less interesting that the story was based on the facts of certain revolutionary activities of the day, than that it was partly written during the Franco-Prussian War of 1870.[2]

The factual background of *The Possessed* lay principally in the notorious murder in 1869 of a young student who had become involved in a revolutionary conspiracy in Moscow, and had tried to free himself from it. Dostoievsky had formed a poor opinion of revolutionaries since his own experience in 1849, and this opinion had been confirmed by a revolutionary congress he attended at Geneva in 1867, of which he wrote that " the absurdity, the feebleness, the mutual contradictions pass all imagining." [3] There had been a slight recrudescence of revolutionary activity in Russia in the 1860's: there was incendiarism in Petersburg in 1862, and an attempt on the life of the Tsar's brother in the same year, and on the Tsar, Alexander II, himself in 1866. These were trivial occurrences compared to the great conspiracy

---

[1] See Dostoievsky's letter to Maikov in Koteliansky, pp. 92–3.

[2] The war is alluded to in a subtle piece of musical irony in *The Possessed*, p. 292.

[3] Carr, p. 175.

which culminated in the assassination of the Tsar a few weeks
after Dostoievsky's death in 1881, but he already saw years
in advance the terrible potentialities of revolution. The full
depth of his vision only became apparent after the Communist
revolution [1] of 1917, or perhaps only in 1949, when the
Soviet Government denounced Dostoievsky as " a wicked,
arrant enemy of the revolution." [2] They were three-quarters
of a century behind the Tsarist Ministry of the Interior, which
made the same gratifying discovery in 1874.[3]

Dostoievsky appreciated, however, as the Tsar's officials
did not, that revolution was a social and not merely a political
phenomenon. *The Possessed* is written at two levels, which
are distinguished by the segregation of the principal characters
into two generations. The social conflict between Liberalism
and reaction revolves round two characters of an older generation : Stepan Trofimovitch, a Liberal of the 1840's who once
wrote a political allegory in verse for which he daily expects
arrest, and Mme Varvara Stavrogin, a domineering woman
with whom he has secretly been in love for twenty years.
The political conflict revolves round their respective sons,
Verhovensky and Stavrogin ; and the pattern is completed
by the reversal of the relationship between the principal
characters in the second generation, Verhovensky attempting
to impose his fanatical will on Stavrogin just as Stavrogin's
mother imposes hers on Verhovensky's father.[4]

Round these principals moves a cluster of satellites. In
the older generation are the local governor's wife and the
pompous novelist Karmazinov (notoriously intended as a

[1] Dostoievsky specifically mentions Communism : *The Possessed*, p. 272.
[2] *The Times*, 21 March 1949.
[3] Carr, p. 232.
[4] This pattern was an afterthought : Dostoievsky admitted at the time
(in a letter to Strakhov, 9 October 1870) that after he had begun the novel
he shifted the role of hero from Stephan Trofimovitch to Stavrogin, that
is from the social to the political level.

parody of Turgenev)[1] who help Mme Stavrogin in organising her *chef d'oeuvre*, a literary and cultural *fête* in aid of the impoverished governesses of the neighbourhood. In the younger generation is the group of revolutionaries whom Verhovensky organises to overthrow society, comprising (by a subtle and perceptive irony) specimens from every type and rank of society except the working-class : the story even introduces a large factory-population for the negatively express purpose of playing no part whatever in the revolution. The connecting link between the social and political activities, which precipitates the *débâcle* of both, is the demonic personality of Stavrogin, a more finished version of Rogozhin from *The Idiot* and of the narrator of *Letters from the Underworld*, as well as a first draft of *The Great Sinner* whose *Life* was never destined to be written. The crux of the story, at which the social and political levels intersect, is made plain in the bewildered question of one of the revolutionaries : " What connection is there between the common cause and the petty intrigues of Mr. Stavrogin ? " [2]

There is no answer intelligible to the revolutionaries, for Stavrogin's character is incomprehensible to all of them, even to Verhovensky who is trying to manipulate him. Verhovensky's revolution would have failed in any case, because the elaborate network of nation-wide cells, of which he claimed to form a part, never existed except in his own imagination ; but as it happened the failure was due to Stavrogin's aloof contempt for the role of figurehead in which Verhovensky had cast him. Stavrogin's character is a perplexing but not an unnatural one : the explanation of it is simple. Given the premiss that a rational man is one who can perceive the moral distinction between good and evil,

---

[1] Yet either by carelessness or to cover up the parody, Dostoievsky once quotes Turgenev under his own name in *The Possessed*, p. 192.

[2] *The Possessed*, p. 494.

Liberal philosophers have always taken it for granted that, other things being equal, the good has only to be recognised to be preferred to the evil. But there sometimes operates an instinctive impulse in rational man to prefer evil though recognising good : Stavrogin is the embodiment of that instinct. He reveals it first in a trivial way, by pulling a respectable old man round the room by his nose merely for saying that no one could lead him by the nose ; he emphasises it by fighting a pointless duel with the old man's son. He seduces a girl brought up in his mother's house, rapes an eleven-year-old child,[1] torments his *fiancée*, and marries an imbecile cripple because " anything more monstrous it was impossible to imagine." Finally he hangs himself, as the last conceivable crime, after allowing Verhovensky's revolutionaries to break up his mother's literary *fête*, as well as their own revolution, in a futile orgy of drunkenness, looting, arson and murder. It is a characteristic irony that Verhovensky's failure is directly due to a genius more evil and more rational than his own.

Yet Verhovensky's revolution is not negligible. He is a ruthless fanatic, capable of murdering one of his followers [2] for trying to secede, and of using the suicide of another [3] to cover the murder. Through his character Dostoievsky gave a solemn, prophetic and terrifyingly detailed prediction of the inevitable course of revolution. Elaborate parallels can be drawn from *The Possessed* with events which happened

[1] This episode does not appear in the published version of *The Possessed*, but there is a separate English version of it called *Stavrogin's Confession* ; the improbable story that it is based on Dostoievsky's own experience is refuted by Carr, p. 114.

[2] Shatov, whose story is based on the *cause célèbre* referred to on p. 51 ; but Shatov is provided with his own biographical background, which curiously anticipates that of Zhelyabov, the organiser of Alexander II's assassination in 1881, whom Dostoievsky never knew.

[3] Kirillov, an epileptic engineer, for whom self-inflicted death was the supreme act of self-assertion.

a generation later.[1] One that is particularly interesting is Dostoievsky's representation of the ringleaders as Russians returning from abroad, as they were indeed to be in 1917, though no one would have expected it in the 1870's; for exiled revolutionaries like Herzen and Bakunin were far easier for Tsarist officials to watch than those like Zhelyabov at home, and even Dostoievsky himself was still under police supervision throughout his years abroad. But it is at least more probable that in representing Stavrogin and Verhovensky, like Prince Myshkin in *The Idiot*, as returning exiles, Dostoievsky was thinking more immediately of his own position.

During his four years abroad his mind was much occupied by the relation of Russia to Western Europe, which he concluded to be wholly advantageous to the latter. Russia, he decided from observation, had nothing to learn from Europe, but Europe everything from Russia; the Russians " are the only god-bearing people on earth "[2] and the Orthodox religion was the only true one. Europe's unforgivable failure lay in its worship of the individual and its blindness to Russia's great discovery that the individual was of no significance except in relation to the group; collectivism was to Dostoievsky (as it still is) an ideal of which only Russians could be fully capable. Having come to these conclusions, he found it impossible to live away from Russia any longer. Besides, exile had done nothing to relieve the load of debt; it had even added the expensive attraction of gambling. By the end of 1870, before *The Possessed* was completed, Anna was pregnant again and anxious to bear her next child in Petersburg. The decision to return suited both of them. On 28 April 1871 Dostoievsky gambled at roulette for the last time in his life;[3] in July they arrived back in Petersburg, and a week later their first son, Fyodor Fyodorovitch (Fedya), was born in rented lodgings.

[1] See p. 99, n. 4. [2] *The Possessed*, p. 223. [3] Anna, p. 136.

CHAPTER IV

TRIUMPH

THE last ten years of Dostoievsky's life were idyllic in comparison with the first fifty. This was partly because he was now a famous author and could assure himself of a steady income, but still more it was thanks to his wife. Without her control over his life, neither fame nor a steady income would have overcome his perennial indebtedness. She made herself not only his business-manager by a formal power of attorney, but also his publisher and eventually even his bookseller; and when his rich aunt Kumanina at last died, after many false alarms, Anna alone succeeded in securing for him his proper share of the estate after a long family squabble. In 1871 she took in her own name a flat for the family in Petersburg, and later a summer home at Staraya Russa on Lake Ilmen. She furnished the flat on the instalment system, again in her own name, so that when his creditors from the distant past caught up with him, there was nothing they could legally seize. She pointed out to them that unless they would accept repayment by small instalments, their only recourse was to put her husband in the debtor's prison, where he would earn nothing. It was soon recognised who was managing the lion.

Her courageous entry into the field of publishing is best described in her own words, which unconsciously suggest that Dostoievsky was as incapable of truly understanding her spirit as she was of penetrating his genius. When the serialisation of *The Possessed* in Katkov's *Russky Vestnik* was finished at the end of 1872, she recorded in her memoirs : [1]

[1] Anna, p. 145–51.

At that time no author published his works himself. . . .
I was indignant that the lion's share of the profit (fifty to
sixty per cent) had to go to the booksellers . . . and I was
thinking how to find a way of selling the books myself and
for cash. . . . I made enquiries in bookshops as to what
discount they got, but I received the vaguest replies. . . .
Once as I was buying a pamphlet I asked the price of a book ;
I was told that it cost four roubles. I purposely asked them
to let me have it for two and a half roubles, on the pretext
that they surely got fifty or sixty per cent discount. The
assistant was indignant and declared that they got only twenty
or twenty-five per cent, and only got thirty per cent on a
very few books. From these enquiries I gathered clearly
what a discount had to be given to the booksellers and how
it varied with the number of copies taken. . . .

After this and similar reconnaissances, Anna launched her
first publishing venture, which was the book-form of *The
Possessed* (referred to as *The Devils*). The first buyer arrived
on the morning of her announcement.

I came out into the hall and asked the man who had sent
him and what he wanted. " We saw your announcement,"
he said, " so I should like to take ten *Devils*." I got out the
copies and with some agitation I said : " The price is thirty-
five roubles, the discount is twenty per cent, so you have to
pay me twenty-eight roubles." " Why such a small discount ?
Can't you make it thirty per cent ? " the man asked. " No,
I cannot." " Well, twenty-five per cent ? " " Really, no,"
I said, but in my own mind I was very uneasy : suppose he
were to go away, and I missed my first customer ? " Well,
if you cannot, then here is the money," and he handed me the
twenty-eight roubles. I was so glad that I gave him thirty
copecs for a cab. . . .

Throughout the remaining years of Dostoievsky's life, and
even long after his death, such scenes were commonplaces

of his wife's daily routine, in addition to bringing up her family. Dostoievsky appreciated little of what she achieved for him, or at what expense : when she told him of the sale of the first hundred and fifteen copies of *The Possessed*, he first laughed at her as if she were joking, and then took the success for granted. Sometimes his complacency exasperated her into a longing to make fun of him, which she did once by an elaborate practical joke designed to provoke his jealousy, with nearly disastrous results.[1] It is clear between the lines of her own account that this was not the only occasion when a certain skittishness on her part failed to chime with his mood ; and the hint is confirmed by a reiterated implication of " untrustworthiness " in her, which is never made specific, at many points in his letters. But even his determination to be the dominant partner could not blind him to the fact that he owed the external tranquillity of his life entirely to Anna.

Thanks to her management he had no need to write in desperate haste again for his bread and butter. The result was to add little to his reputation for many years, though in the end his comparative leisure was justified by its final fruit. For five years he amused himself with journalism : first he edited a journal called *Grazhdanin* for an adventurer called Prince Meshchersky ; later he launched an independent periodical of his own called *A Writer's Diary*, in which he set out his views on many different topics and occasionally included a few short stories. During this period he undertook only one novel, and that only on the invitation of a rival editor, who was none other than his first admirer, Nekrasov. Their relations had been strained ever since Dostoievsky broke away from Byelinsky's circle in 1847 ; but in 1874 Nekrasov called on Dostoievsky on his own initiative, and with Anna's enthusiastic approval it was agreed that a full-length novel should be written for his journal. The

[1] See Anna, pp. 158 *seqq.*

editorship of *Grazhdanin* was terminated, and Katkov's formal permission to work for another editor was secured—an innovation in Dostoievsky's etiquette which may be attributed to Anna, though Katkov's readiness was rather due to the fact that he had just arranged with Tolstoy to publish *Anna Karenina*. Then Dostoievsky was carried off to Staraya Russa to write *A Raw Youth* at his leisure in 1874–5.

The result was disappointing. *A Raw Youth* (which might be called in English less clumsily *The Adolescent* or *The Awkward Age*, but has been called even more clumsily *The Hobbledehoy*) is a patchwork which never succeeds in revealing a pattern. The ingredients are Dostoievsky's memories of his own adolescence, no doubt as inaccurate as most such memories are, combined with substantial drafts from his notes on *The Life of a Great Sinner* and a melodramatic plot which culminates in a forced climax of almost inextricable nonsense. Subjectively the story is about the struggle of a nineteen-year-old boy to achieve spiritual harmony with his father, who is another but less successful version of the rational will to evil. Objectively the story is about a tangle of social intrigue, turning upon two compromising letters which are always falling into the wrong hands, besides apparently getting muddled with each other in Dostoievsky's own mind. The clumsiness of the narrative is largely due to the fact that throughout the " raw youth " is himself the narrator, so that he is obliged either to guess at things he could know nothing about, or to spend chapters at a time accidentally overhearing other people's conversations. He does both, and the result is ludicrous. It has been well said of *A Raw Youth* that " whilst it progresses one feels the shattering bumps of a badly sprung carriage on an interminable journey." [1] This was Dostoievsky's last attempt to tell a story through the eyes of a principal participant, and it is by

[1] Meier-Graefe, D., *The Man and His Work*, p. 282.

far the least successful.[1] Writing at leisure was apparently not, in spite of all his and Anna's complaints, a sure way for Dostoievsky to produce masterpieces.

The precedent of his earlier career suggests that in the middle 1870's he had not enough anxieties to be a great novelist. His worries were comparatively few and trivial. There were occasional editorial troubles, which once cost him a few days of formal imprisonment for an accidental breach of the censorship ; there were recurrent quarrels with his relations, and particularly the odious conduct of his stepson Pasha ; there was the continuation of police surveillance almost to the end of his life ; there was endless correspondence, which Dostoievsky enjoyed though it distracted him from work, with young students who now looked on him as an oracle ; there was the undignified jealousy he felt towards both Turgenev and Tolstoy, his only living rivals who were still set above him in commercial esteem ; and finally there were periodical separations from Anna, brought about by the exigencies of his health. The trouble was no longer his epilepsy, which was tending to diminish in violence, but a chronic catarrh for which he had to take a yearly cure at Ems in Germany. Because Anna had to stay behind with the children, the youngest of whom was born in 1875, the years 1874-9 are relatively rich in letters ; and these are eked out by other short separations, for instance when Anna was at Staraya Russa and he in Petersburg.

His correspondence makes very commonplace reading. The letters from Ems are full of his utter distaste for Germany, which he described soberly and repeatedly as worse than Siberia ; of his trivial adventures and financial anxieties ; of

---

[1] *The Possessed* was formally narrated in the first person, and so was *The Brothers Karamazov* to be later ; but in neither case is the narrator an important participant in the action, and Dostoievsky often forgot him altogether.

his passion for Anna and his family. When he found himself
alone with his elder son, he would solemnly record such
triumphant simplicities as : [1]

> "I asked Fedya yesterday : 'Where is Mother now ?'
> He thought for a minute and then answered—very solemnly :
> 'I don't know.'"

To Anna he wrote with a frank passion which led her to
expurgate many of his letters before. publication. What is
left is revealing of the childishness of genius :

> Again I kiss you a thousand times. It is possible to kiss a
> thousand times, but to write as you do, that you kiss me
> 10,000,000 times is obviously a lie. It is easy to write down
> noughts, but in actual fact. . . .

As he had himself written a few months before that he kissed
her 50,355 times, and at other occasions a million times, it
would be interesting to know where he drew the line.

His longer letters from Ems, by their very triviality, give
a vivid picture of the sort of being whom it was Anna's cross
and pride to look after. Once he wrote in agony of three
"troublesome adventures," of which the first was the loss of
a shirt ("I don't think it was one of my best"), the third
was being kept awake by Jews in the next room at his hotel
(". . . they squeal as if they were in an Israelitic consistorium
or a synagogue . . .") and the second and most terrible was
this : [2]

> Two days ago, on Saturday, I went to gargle my throat.
> I went in the room where fifty places are arranged for gargling,
> and I put my umbrella in the corner, and on going out of the
> room I forgot it. A quarter of an hour later, I missed it ;
> I went back for it, but could not find it ; someone had taken
> it. It had been raining all night and all morning and I thought

[1] Hill and Mudie, p. 148.   [2] *Op. cit.*, p. 268.

to myself : it is Sunday to-morrow ; the shops will be closed
and what shall I do if it rains ? I went and bought another,
a very bad one it seems, a silk one of course, costing 14 marks
(6 roubles in our money). After selling it to me, the shopkeeper (a crafty Jew) said : " Have you made enquiries about
your umbrella at the police ? " " Where can you find the
police in the Kursaal ? " " Oh, there *is* a department there."
And I didn't know it. I went and asked them, and my
umbrella was immediately returned to me, they had found it
long ago. How amazing ! I offered the wretched shopkeeper
2 marks if he would take the new umbrella back and return
the 12 marks to me, but he refused. It's absolutely tragic how
money simply runs away here.

Even this was not quite so tragic as in the days of roulette
at Homburg ; but if Anna had been there, it might not have
seemed quite so amazing that the lost umbrella was not lost
for ever.

It is noteworthy that the story is not even particularly well
told ; and that is characteristic of Dostoievsky's letters, which
are often exceedingly long and must have occupied hours of
his time, and yet remain hardly worth reading for their own
sakes. Just occasionally a glimpse of the natural story-teller
breaks through the clouds of verbiage, as in this example,
which was also written from Ems : [1]

At dawn, before we reached Giessen I saw a picture of shame
in real life. The train had stopped for ten minutes, and as we
had not stopped for a long time, everybody naturally ran off
to a certain place labelled " Gentlemen," and just at the
busiest time there ran into the place, which was crowded
with about twenty people, a lady, beautifully dressed, and
judging from her appearance, an Englishwoman. She was
probably in a great hurry, because she ran into the middle
of the place before she realised her mistake, *i.e.* that she had

[1] Hill and Mudie, p. 206.

gone into "Gentlemen" instead of the place next door labelled "Ladies." She suddenly stopped, thunderstruck, and then with a look of utter horror and terrified amazement, which didn't last for more than a second, she gave a very loud cry or rather a scream, just as you scream when you suddenly get a fright ; then she clapped her hands together, raised them above her head and we all heard the sound of clapping. She must have seen everything, *i.e.* absolutely everything, for no one had time to cover himself. On the contrary, we all looked at her like dummies. Then she quickly covered her face with both hands, turned round slowly (the worst had happened, there was no need to hurry any more !) and bending forward with her whole body, without hurrying and not without dignity, she left the place. I don't know whether she went into the place for "Ladies," but if she was an Englishwoman, I think she must have died there and then for shame. The surprising part of it all was that there was absolutely no laughter at all, the Germans were all glum and silent, whereas in Russia there would probably have been a burst of laughter and a guffaw of delight.

But this sort of entertainment is rare in his letters from abroad : they are nine-tenths filled with domestic problems, the state of his health, the horror of life abroad, the law-suit over the Kumanin inheritance, and the prospects of a fresh advance from Katkov.

These minor agitations show by themselves that he had no major anxieties on his mind. His fiery temperament was burning lower, and his writings no longer bore the marks of the furnace. Even when his younger son died in 1878, of an inherited epilepsy at the age of three, the tragedy evoked nothing to compare with the agony of wild grief that poured out over the death of his first child Sonia ten years before. But the journeys abroad did serve to revive in Dostoievsky's mind one of the most fanatical of his earlier themes, the place of Russia in Europe. This time his conviction of the superiority of all things Russian was rather unreasonably bolstered by the perilous success with which Tsarist foreign policy encouraged the rising of the Slav peoples in the Balkans in 1875, which culminated in war between Russia and Turkey in 1877. The Tsarist government momentarily succeeded in upsetting the balance of power in the Balkans by enlarging Bulgaria at the Treaty of San Stefano in 1878, but this achievement was quickly upset by the other European powers at the Congress of Berlin later in the year. There could be no doubt which side Dostoievsky was on in this struggle. His growing fame had brought him the friendship of the Tsar's powerful minister Pobedonostsev, and even the Tsarevitch himself was an admirer of his novels.[1] Bursting with loyalty and nationalism, Dostoievsky poured out through the pages of *A Writer's Diary* such torrents of mystical jingoism as had rarely been heard before. He predicted the extinction of England and France in a pan-European blood-bath, which would leave Holy Russia in occupation of Constantinople, and the Slav peoples (except, of course, the renegade Poles, who were incorrigible) as masters of all Europe. It is questionable how much of this Dostoievsky really believed, and how much was a concession to public opinion and his friends at court. But at least the enthusiastic energy he put into it suggests that he found in this outlet a substitute for his thwarted passion for gambling.[2]

The rest of *A Writer's Diary* is made up of Dostoievsky's views on many different topics of the day, such as litigation (of which Mme Kumanina's legacy had given him bitter experience) and the feminist question (in which he was strongly

[1] See Koteliansky, pp. 239 *seqq.* : the Tsarevitch was later Alexander III.
[2] Anna is usually given all the credit for Dostoievsky's abandonment of roulette ; but some should surely be given to the German federal authorities, who closed all public gambling-houses in 1872, and drove their managers to seek refuge and rehabilitation at Monto Carlo.

on the women's side) ; but it also includes a few short stories, which Mrs. Constance Garnett extracted for inclusion in his collected fiction. None of them is of major importance, except indirectly *The Peasant Marey* for biographical reasons which have already been discussed ;[1] but *A Gentle Spirit* deserves to be read as perhaps the best short story he ever wrote. It describes the spiritual cruelty of a man with an inferiority complex towards a girl whom he has at his mercy, finally driving her to suicide. Almost alone among Dostoievsky's short stories, it suggests that the *genre* was not wholly foreign to his genius. But the other stories published during the same years were little more than pot-boilers to fill up space. *Bobok* is a macabre dialogue overheard in a graveyard between corpses in their tombs ; *The Heavenly Christmas Tree* is a sentimental fragment about the homeless orphan whom Dostoievsky borrowed many years before from Dickens, written as if merely to keep his hand in with the type ; and *The Dream of a Ridiculous Man* is primarily an evocation of an imaginary paradise, which may well owe something to the Dream of *Oblomov* in Goncharov's novel. Indeed, many of the short stories of this period are under suspicion of having been borrowed from elsewhere, and none need be taken seriously.

There is in fact only one more work of Dostoievsky's life to be taken seriously, and that so seriously as to be called his life-work in itself, for everything that went before seems only to pave the way to it. During all the years that Dostoievsky appeared to waste on lightweight fiction and jingo journalism, *The Life of a Great Sinner* was never out of his mind. It was still never to be written, for Dostoievsky contemplated at least another ten more years [2] of activity than fate allowed

---

[1] See p. 14 above.

[2] He estimated twenty years in a letter less than three months before his death (Koteliansky, *New D. Letters*, p. 100).

him. But in 1877 he bestirred himself to draw on the project for another stupendous effort of writing. The moment of its inception has been tentatively assigned to the summer of 1877, when he was unable to go abroad because of the war, and visited instead the farm in the province of Tula, which his father had bought nearly fifty years before, and which was now occupied by his sister Vera. If the idea of the new novel came to him then, it was certainly fertilised by a friendship which sprang up about the same time between Dostoievsky and the young philosopher Soloviev. Dostoievsky attended his lectures on philosophy early in 1878, and together they visited a famous monastery in the province of Tula. The visit made a deep impression on Dostoievsky. The result was the first few chapters of *The Brothers Karamazov*, which Katkov began to serialise in *Russky Vestnik* at the beginning of 1879.

The external action of *The Brothers Karamazov* is the easiest of all his novels to describe, simply because it is the culmination of his movement away from the novel of incident towards the novel of character. There is therefore less incident than in any other novel, though it is much the longest of them ; what action there is moves simply, compactly and dramatically. The function of this action is merely to provide an external background to the interplay of character : in speaking of the catastrophe he is about to introduce, Dostoievsky explicitly adds " or rather, the external side of it." [1] This catastrophe, which is the murder of the revolting old monster, Karamazov, springs from his relationship with his sons : Dmitri, the son of his first wife ; Ivan and Alyosha, the sons of his second ; and Smerdyakov, his valet, the illegitimate son of an imbecile girl whom he raped in a drunken orgy. Dmitri, who shares old Karamazov's earthy sensuality, hates his father for squandering his inheritance ; Ivan also hates him, in a more dispas-

[1] *The Brothers Karamazov*, p. 7.

sionate, intellectual, inactive way ; and Smerdyakov is little more than a crafty animal, subject to epileptic fits and crazy ideas. But Alyosha is a saint : it was his intention to spend his life in a monastery, if he had not been sent out into the world by his dying elder, Father Zossima, to act as a spiritual cushion between the deadly nature of the Karamazovs and their fellow-men.

There are four cases in particular where Alyosha's saintliness is needed to mitigate the effects of what Dostoievsky calls " the Karamazov nature." One is the monastery itself, with which old Karamazov is engaged in a bitter law-suit : this provides the occasion for a meeting of the whole family with Father Zossima, during which the murder of the father is first predicted. The second case is that of a notorious courtesan, Grushenka, for whom Dmitri and his father are rivals ; the father offers her three thousand roubles (of what Dmitri considers to be his money) if she will come to him. The third case is a proud and wealthy girl, Katerina, who is in love alternately with Dmitri and Ivan ; but her supposed love for Dmitri is no more than gratitude for a debt of honour she owes him from the past. The last case, a little apart from the rest, is a group of schoolboys, one of whom suffers deeply from the humiliation of an insult perpetrated without motive by Dmitri on his father. Alyosha's success in winning the confidence of this group of boys is counterbalanced by the temptation into which he is led by the sexual precocity of a crippled girl of fourteen ; and these episodes, which form only a side-issue in *The Brothers Karamazov*, were intended to be the precursors of a sequel (or perhaps more than one) in which Alyosha himself was to have been the tragic hero, and perhaps even to have become *The Great Sinner* himself.

All the events, in which Alyosha tries to play his part of mitigating the force of inevitable evil, culminate in the murder

of old Karamazov, as Father Zossima predicted on his deathbed. Suspicion of the murder is divided between Dmitri
and Smerdyakov : Dmitri, because he visited his father's
house that night and knocked out his servant in the garden
with a brass pestle, which might also have been the instrument
that killed old Karamazov ; and Smerdyakov, because he
was the only possible alternative in the neighbourhood of
the house, though he appeared to be in the aftermath of an
epileptic fit at the time of the murder. The case turns on the
disappearance of the three thousand roubles which old
Karamazov had promised Grushenka. On the night of the
murder, Dmitri is caught in an orgy with Grushenka on money
which he had not had a few hours before. He contends that
the money came from a sum entrusted to him some weeks
before by Katerina, of which he had already squandered half
but intended to return the other half. No one believes him
except his intimates, because everyone believes that he had
already squandered the whole of Katerina's money in a previous
orgy. But he is telling the truth ; and on the night
before the trial, Smerdyakov confesses to Ivan that he
is the murderer, and hands over the three thousand
roubles which he took from his dead master. The same
night he hangs himself.

Yet this is not the climax. Ivan goes mad from a guilty
conscience, convinced that Smerdyakov committed the
murder at his instigation. Katerina, heartbroken at Ivan's
collapse, gives unexpected evidence at the trial which appears
conclusive of Dmitri's guilt. Dmitri accepts his condemnation
to Siberia with enthusiasm, insisting that he is suffering on
behalf of all humanity, and that he deserves to suffer not
because he was the murderer of his father but because he was
" a scoundrel " towards Katerina. Grushenka accompanies
him to Siberia (not without a conviction that they are going
to escape on the way), and Alyosha delivers a deeply moving

epilogue at the funeral with which the novel ends. But it is not the funeral of old Karamazov : it is the funeral of the boy whose father Dmitri insulted, the most pathetic of all the victims of " the Karamazov nature."

These are the external events of one of the greatest novels ever written. Their internal meaning belongs to Dostoievsky's own spiritual biography, which must be the subject of another chapter. This internal meaning is displayed not only in the external events themselves, their sequence and interrelation, but even more in the long passages which are rather interpolated commentaries on the action. The chief of these are, firstly, the chapters called *The Grand Inquisitor*,[1] in which Ivan explains allegorically to Alyosha his reasons for rejecting Christianity as it has historically developed ; secondly, the chapters giving Father Zossima's biography,[2] which describes the genesis of a saint ; and thirdly, the speeches at Dmitri's trial,[3] which are long philosophical disquisitions containing no new facts about the murder. Much the most important of the three is the first, a brilliantly ironic development of the theme that if Christ returned to earth he would be in danger of being sentenced to death again as a rebel by his own followers ; but on the whole, too much importance has been attached to the supposed symbolism of the story, and too little to the fact that Dostoievsky blatantly weights the scales by representing Christ as returning to earth at Seville " in the most terrible time of the Inquisition." It would be fairer to interpret the legend as yet another of Dostoievsky's attacks on the Roman Catholic Church, which he regarded as the greatest force for evil in the world.

The completion of this novel in 1880 made Dostoievsky a legendary figure in his lifetime. The benign influence of Anna converted him into a literary lion. There is a charming

[1] *The Brothers Karamazov*, pp. 253 *seqq.*   [2] *Op. cit.*, pp. 295 *seqq.*
[3] *Op. cit.*, pp. 735 *seqq.*

picture of him in this year, to be found in Anna's memoirs, going out to perform at literary *soirées* under her escort : [1]

> I always took with me to these evenings the volume from which my husband was to read, along with Ems pastilles—a remedy for his cough—a spare handkerchief (in case he lost his), a plaid to wrap up his neck on his coming out into the cold air, and so on. Seeing me always so equipped, Fyodor used to call me his " faithful armour-bearer."

There was no question that it was all done by kindness, for Dostoievsky thoroughly enjoyed the performance. This is evident from his own account of the most celebrated episode in his career as a literary lion, which took place in Moscow on 8 June 1880, at the unveiling of a statue of Pushkin. Because Anna could not accompany him, and because the ceremony was several times delayed, a series of thirteen letters survives giving Dostoievsky's own account of this curious occasion, which at the time eclipsed even *The Brothers Karamazov* in public esteem.

It was doubtful at first how well the ceremony would go, because Tolstoy was not there, and Turgenev, who was to speak before Dostoievsky, was still unreconciled to him. There were several days of intrigue and counter-intrigue about the conduct of the proceedings, and Dostoievsky's turn did not come until the third day of the actual festival. But then, in the words of his first biographer, Strakhov, " everyone began to listen as if nobody had yet said anything about Pushkin." The theme of Dostoievsky's speech was mainly that Pushkin's universal genius transcended such petty squabbles as those still exercising Russia between Westerners and Slavophils. The outcome of it was that the two factions, including Turgenev himself, declared themselves reconciled

[1] Anna, p. 172, note.

there and then in the lecture hall. Dostoievsky wrote to
Anna the same afternoon : [1]

> When at the end I proclaimed the *universal union* of people,
> the hall was as though in hysterics, and when I finished,—
> I cannot tell you about the roar, about the wail of ecstasy :
> strangers among the public cried, wept, embraced one another,
> *and swore to one another to be better, not to hate one another from*
> *henceforth, but to love.*

Independent accounts confirm Dostoievsky's words with
ample detail : a student fainted at his feet, a group of ladies
crowned him with a wreath of flowers, applause stopped
the ceremony, and even Turgenev blew him a kiss. But
when the speech was published later in the year, in *A Writer's
Diary*, the reaction had already set in. It was critically
attacked by rivals who had not been present at the delivery,
and many who had been present began to feel that they had
somehow been defrauded, for the substance of the argument
proved to be very thin. Dostoievsky was bitterly disappointed
by the end of the year ; yet the nature of his triumph at the
time proves that at least the personality of his genius was not
played out. This last episode of his literary life confirms
what his last novel so strongly suggests : that although *The
Brothers Karamazov* was the summit of his achievement, it
was not the consummation of his life's work in the sense
that he had nothing more to say.

He was already planning a further decade of work when
the year 1881 began. But late on Sunday, 25 January, after
an exhausting day which included a quarrel with his sisters
about the inheritance of their aunt Kumanina, he burst an
artery in the lung and suffered from a severe hæmorrhage
the next day. By 28 January he was convinced that he was
dying, and found confirmation of the belief in a phrase

[1] Koteliansky, p. 232.

picked out at random from the Bible which he had carried
with him ever since his days in Siberia.   He died that evening,
while Anna successfully kept his stepson Pasha at bay ; only
she and his children and Maikov were present at the end.
The funeral was a great public event in Petersburg, and the
first speech over the grave was made by one of the few
survivors who had stood with Dostoievsky at the mock
execution in 1849.   The Tsar Alexander II granted Anna a
pension of 2000 roubles a year : four weeks later he was
dead himself, assassinated by a group of men whose coming
Dostoievsky had foreseen ten years earlier in *The Possessed*.

CHAPTER V

AUTOBIOGRAPHY

IT was said at the beginning of the first chapter that
Dostoievsky was an intensely autobiographical novelist;
and also that to him the inner history of the spirit was
of incomparably greater importance than the external history
of his physical life. In the absence of any formal autobiography from his pen, facts relating to the latter proposition
can only be deduced from his fiction and journalism. But
the validity of these deductions will rest largely on the truth
of the first proposition, which therefore needs to be
independently established. Now that the external facts of
his life have been briefly summarised, there will be no difficulty
in illustrating this fact, that in the later part of his life, at
least, his own experiences were constantly in his mind when
he was writing fiction.

There are certain major examples for which no proof is
needed : *The House of the Dead* and *The Gambler*, for instance,
have almost the authenticity of a diary, though both are cast
in the form of fiction. Only a little way behind them stands
A Raw Youth, which avowedly draws upon the unhappiness
of Dostoievsky's schooldays, and adds to them, like *The
Gambler*, his later passion for roulette, including his explicitly
stated conviction that the infallible way to win was " simply
to keep calm." Of the short stories, only *The Peasant Marey*
is intentionally autobiographical throughout, even if it rests
on no more than the recollection of a hallucination. The
remarkable case of *White Nights* should be added as an
example of Dostoievsky's life following his fiction instead of

vice versa, since the narrator of the story helped his beloved into the arms of his rival nearly a decade before Dostoievsky undertook to do the same for Maria Isayev. But the importance of this example is that it is not only inverted but unique ; there is perhaps no other case to be quoted of any precise relation of resemblance either way between Dostoievsky's writings and his life in the pre-Siberian period.

After his release from Siberia, however, his fiction became increasingly egocentric. One of the first instances is the same theme as that of *White Nights* : the theme which he had copied from his early short story into his life was copied back again into his first full-length novel, *The Insulted and Injured*, and recurs intermittently afterwards. But much more important examples soon eclipsed it. The theme of a man's thoughts on his way to execution occupies many pages of *The Idiot* ; the arrest of Stepan Trofimovitch in *The Possessed* repeats Dostoievsky's own experience in 1849, even to the suggestion that one member of the family was arrested by mistake for another ;[1] the death-scene of Marmeladov's wife in *Crime and Punishment* is said by Dostoievsky's second wife to be based on the death of his first ;[2] the onset of epilepsy is repeatedly described from experience ; and so on. The series of coincidences is so remarkable that episodes from the novels have even been extracted and ascribed to his own life without any independent evidence. One of these is the notorious rape of an eleven-year-old girl from *Stavrogin's Confession*. It is easy enough to believe that this was attached to his name by mere association, and adopted deliberately by malicious detractors,[3] when we read on Dostoievsky's own

[1] *The Possessed*, pp. 389–90.

[2] Anna, p. 265. Many more instances can be picked out from her annotations of the novels in the following pages of the same book.

[3] Including his first biographer, Strakhov, in a letter to Tolstoy : see Carr, p. 113.

authority in *The Peasant Marey* that many people believed him to have been sent to Siberia for murdering his wife, merely because that is the crime he attributed to the imaginary narrator of *The House of the Dead*.

These instances are sufficient to establish the general framework of autobiographical tendency in Dostoievsky's fiction, since even the exceptions mentioned in the last sentence, prove the rule in the most rigorous sense of that axiom. But still more remarkable are the trivial instances, often unrelated to the main course of the story, which casually embellish every few pages of the novels. A complete list would be impossible, but half a dozen examples can be given almost at random. From his own youth came the recollection of his father hunting under his sisters' beds for concealed lovers, which reappears in *The Idiot*.[1] A more macabre example from his childhood is the choice of an epitaph for his mother's tomb : the chosen phrase, " Lie here, beloved dust, until the joyful dawn," was later used not only in *The Idiot* (of a man who buried his leg in a cemetery and put up this epitaph over it), but also in *Bobok*, on the tombstone of one of the corpses whose conversation makes up the short story.[2] From the days of his first marriage comes the episode in *Crime and Punishment*, when Marmeladov's wife accepts three roubles as charity after his death, just as Maria Isayev was said to have done in Siberia after her first husband's death and before her marriage to Dostoievsky.[3] From his gambling days comes the episode, to be found both in *The Gambler* and in *A Raw Youth*, of a roulette player accidentally provoking a quarrel by picking up another player's money, as Dostoievsky once did himself.[4] From the period between his marriages comes the scene in *The Idiot* in which Prince Myshkin interrupts a genteel tea-party with a violent denunciation of

[1] See above, p. 17.   [2] See Mackiewicz, p. 140.
[3] See Mackiewicz, p. 70.   [4] Anna, p. 88.

mothers who try to dispose of their daughters to the highest
bidder, just as Dostoievsky once denounced Mme Korvin-
Krukovskaya for having the same intentions at a time when
he was interested in her daughter.[1] From his own experience
of the loss of his baby Sonia, finally, comes this moving
passage from *The Brothers Karamazov*.[2]

> Many years pass by, and he has other children and loves
> them. But how could he love those new ones when those
> first children are no more, when he has lost them? Remember-
> ing them, how could he be fully happy with those new ones,
> however dear the new ones might be? But he could, he
> could. It's the great mystery of human life that old grief
> passes gradually into quiet tender joy. . . .

The last example, which is taken from a sermon by Father
Zossima on the subject of Job, illustrates the culmination of a
habit of thought, to which all the others belong at an earlier
stage. It was Dostoievsky's tendency, even when drawing
on his own experience, to be interested not in the realistic
presentation of the episode, but in its inner content. None
of the episodes described in this brief list of parallels is a
merely photographic reproduction, nor are the characters
concerned in them direct portraits from life. This is a
significant point of technique, which requires a short discussion
on Dostoievsky's method of characterisation. For almost
every reader of his novels is inclined to agree that, although
his characters appear to be organically consistent within
themselves and to grow throughout their stories logically
along the lines laid down for them,[3] nevertheless they are
unlike any recognisable human beings in their external

[1] Carr, p. 130.   [2] *The Brothers Karamazov*, p. 301.
[3] Alfred Adler (*Individual Psychology*, p. 288) gives a professional
psychologist's testimony to the " integrated unity " of Dostoievsky's
characters.

behaviour. This is equally true of those drawn partially from his experience and of those drawn wholly from his imagination ; but the former provide the easier clues to the understanding of his technique.

Dostoievsky himself anticipated the criticism to be made of his characters, that " people just are not like that and do not behave like that." He gave it expression through the mouth of General Epanchin, one of the few unquestionably normal beings in his works by any standards.[1] After a rather exceptionally chaotic episode in the life of his family, the general remarked unhappily to Prince Myshkin :

> " You're all such queer people. . . . How is it to be explained, do you suppose, except that half of it is mirage, unreal, something like moonshine or some hallucination ? "

This puts very clearly the ordinary man's reaction to Dostoievsky's more important characters : it is perhaps the same as the ordinary man's reaction to Picasso's portraits. True, no woman ever looked exactly like Picasso painted her, in the sense that if you photographed one of his models the result would not be a reproduction of one of his paintings ; but the same is true (with a difference only of degree) of any painter who has ever portrayed human beings, except those academicians who have aimed simply at a speaking likeness in glorious Technicolor. And just as Picasso did not set out to paint covers for chocolate boxes, so Dostoievsky did not set out to write books to be read by General Epanchin. Yet his characters must be recognisably human, or they could not be criticised for being abnormal.

Certainly Dostoievsky's characters do not act, talk or think like typical Anglo-Saxons. This has led to the dangerous fallacy [2] that they act, talk and think like typical Russians.

[1] *The Idiot*, p. 348.   [2] See, *e.g.*, Zweig, *Three Masters*, p. 148.

The truth is that they are not typical anything, because they are not types. They are made up of human characteristics, and even of typical characteristics, but not by way of photographic reproduction. Some of them, it is true, such as General Epanchin and Gavril in *The Idiot*, or Raskolnikov's mother and sister in *Crime and Punishment*, are made up of perfectly normal aggregations of human characteristics ; but others, and by far the most important, such as Rogozhin, Raskolnikov, Stavrogin and Ivan Karamazov, are so constructed and visualised as to appear just as remote and inexplicable to the normal characters, among whom they move, as they do to ourselves. Both the method of construction and the method of visualising them are important, firstly as technique and secondly for the purpose they are designed to serve.

The simplest way to approach the fourfold problem stated in the last sentence is to take first the technique of visualising the characters : in other words, to examine Dostoievsky's peculiar vision. This vision may be compared to that of a curved lens, which exaggerates and even distorts some areas of its field, and leaves other areas of the same field unrefracted in their normal proportions. The purpose and principle of its selection are another matter ; but the metaphor itself is perhaps illuminating enough to be worth enlarging.

If you look at a postage stamp under a magnifying glass, you see its whole surface at once within the circumference of the glass, all more or less uniformly magnified. But if you look at a page of a book, or at any other area larger in extent than the lens, you see only a section of it magnified in isolation within the circumference of the glass ; the rest of the page, although contiguous in your field of vision, is seen on a normal scale which does not fit the magnified area. This trick is familiar in modern advertising : an object is shown on a normal scale, with one section of it picked out on a larger scale within a circle (representing the magnifying glass or lens of a microscope) ; and the neighbouring sections on two different scales adjoin without cohering in the same visual plane, yet are correctly interpreted as parts of the same picture. This, metaphorically speaking, is how Dostoievsky created his characters, on two different scales according to their position in his pictures : enlarged in the foreground, reduced in the background. It is much the same technique as that employed by early painters, who distinguished the figures in the background by simply painting them smaller in the same plane as the figures in the foreground. It is a technique which can only be called primitive by those who realise that the term has no connotation of inability or failure to achieve the sophistications of perspective : it is simply what Dostoievsky preferred.

The technique is at first unfamiliar to English readers because it was foreign to English writers in Dostoievsky's day, and still largely remains so. The difference, which extends to the theatre and can easily be seen in a comparison between (say) Chekhov's *The Cherry Orchard* and any English comedy of manners, is that the English writer distinguishes the foreground and background of his characterisation not by drawing some of his characters on a different scale from the rest, but by filling some of them out with more detailed content and some with less. Suppose you put two groups of foreground and background characters from (say) Thackeray and Dostoievsky under the magnifying glass together. There would be nothing to choose between the outstanding characters of the foreground in either case : Dostoievsky's happen to live permanently under his magnifying glass, but Thackeray's can be put under it beside them without losing reality, depth and outline. The difference comes in the background : in the English writer the background characters have the same

scale as the foreground, but less content ; in Dostoievsky
they have just as rich a content but on a smaller scale. As a
result, the English characters would emerge under the magnifying lens as empty, confused, shapeless smears of colour ;
but the Russians emerge as potentially capable of becoming
heroes and heroines of their respective stories. Dostoievsky
allowed no characters to be mere " extras."

That this is not an academic exercise in hypercriticism is
shown by the fact that it is exactly what happened while
Dostoievsky was writing *The Possessed*.[1] He admitted himself
that Stavrogin grew from being a minor character in the first
part to becoming the major hero halfway through. In the
same way Svidrigailov, whose name is only casually mentioned
towards the beginning of *Crime and Punishment*, slipped under
the microscope and almost ousted Raskolnikov from the
position of protagonist later in the book. The surprising
thing is only that what happened in *The Possessed* did not
happen more often. That particular novel is bursting with
background characters pushing and shoving each other to
get under the lens, any one of whom could have become the
principal figure in the foreground with a little luck. For
several pages at a time the main action is held up while completely irrelevant anecdotes are poured out of Dostoievsky's
inexhaustible mind, about characters who never reappear.[2]
They are sketches for the foreground of still unwritten
masterpieces.

Magnification of the figures in the foreground, however,
creates of itself a further distinction between them and those
of the background. It reveals the natural contradictions
latent in all human character, which do not appear in figures

[1] See his letter to Strakhov, 9 October 1870 (Mayne pp. 209–10).

[2] The *reductio ad absurdum* of this technique occurs in *A Raw Youth*,
where Chapter III, § 4, of Part III consists of a long anecdote which might
almost be written off as interpolated by a printer's blunder.

seen on the smaller scale of " real life " because they merge
into each other.[1]   These are the inconsistencies which led
Walt Whitman to observe unapologetically :

> " Do I contradict myself ?
> Very well then I contradict myself,
> (I am large, I contain multitudes.) "

The effect can be illustrated by the analogy of Impressionist
painting.   If you look at an Impressionist picture from close
up, you see that its colours are really made up of their primary
components, juxtaposed in tiny spots which conflict with
each other when they are seen on such a scale.   If you look
at the picture from a distance, your eye recomposes the conflicting spots into colours of purer shades than those which
come out of a tube of paint.   But you cannot look at a picture
both from a distance and from close up at the same time.
Yet, as the metaphor of the lens has shown, that is just what
Dostoievsky was trying to make his readers do.   He thereby
set himself a problem for which the Impressionists' technique
did not provide a complete solution.

The juxtaposed contrasts and conflicts, of which the
magnifying glass shows the human character to be made up,
would become intolerable to the reader if he had to see them
from close up the whole time ;   in fact, he would never see
the character in its entirety at all.   Dostoievsky solved the
problem in the case of his foreground characters by carrying
the Impressionists' technique a stage further.   To continue
the metaphor :   he not merely separated his colours into their
primary components ;   he transferred the conflicting components to another part of the canvas, so that he had two
studies of the same subject, each coherent in itself and in total
conflict with the other.   This may be offered as an explanation

---

[1] Dostoievsky made this point himself in *The Idiot*, p. 450.   His metaphor
is that " in actual life typical characteristics are apt to be watered down."

of the phenomenon which every critic of Dostoievsky has
pointed out in his works : that many of his characters are
split into two personalities, each the *alter ego* or *doppelgänger*
of the other. An elementary form of the technique appears
in *The Double*, where the dichotomy seems crude and almost
pointless, especially when it is compared with Stevenson's
Dr. Jekyll and Mr. Hyde, which displays this particular trick
to perfection. In Dostoievsky's later work the division is
more subtly made : for instance, in the segregation of the
murderer in *Crime and Punishment* into the rather lovable
Raskolnikov and the entirely loathsome Svidrigailov ; or
more openly in *The Brothers Karamazov*, where Ivan recognises
the Devil, who visits him at the end, as the suppressed double
of himself.[1] It is perhaps possible even to see the mechanism
at work in *The Idiot*, where Myshkin's love is divided between
two aspects of the same feminine compound, Aglaia and
Nastasya ; and the compound is itself made up of Dostoievsky's
dual experience of Anna Korvin-Krukovskaya and Martha
Brown, so that neither can be exclusively identified with
either heroine in the novel.[2]

The most subtle and complex examples of this fissiparous
characterisation are in *The Brothers Karamazov* and *The
Possessed*, a fact perhaps not unconnected with the primacy
which these two novels are generally assigned in Dostoievsky's
achievement. In the former, what he himself calls " the
broad Karamazov character " [3] is split up into no less than
five separate components, represented by the brothers Dmitri,
Ivan, Alyosha, together with Smerdyakov and old Karamazov

[1] *The Brothers Karamazor*, p. 681.

[2] Indeed, characteristically, the relation between Aglaia and Nastasya
even includes one episode from another part of Dostoievsky's life : the
correspondence between them (*The Idiot*, pp. 426–7) is based on a correspondence which he believed to have taken place between his second wife
and Apollinaria Suslova. See Carr, p. 160.

[3] *The Brothers Karamazov*, p. 742.

himself. In *The Possessed* the quadrangular pattern of the four chief characters has already been indicated,[1] and they are all differentiations of the same protoplasm. Not only is the original Stavrogin-character divided between the mother Varvara and her son, and the Verhovensky-character divided between the father Stepan Trofimovitch and his son ; but also the impact of these two characters upon each other is divided into a relation between the two parents on the social level, exactly matched by a converse relation between the two sons on the political level. On both levels the conflict ends in death : in the older generation Stepan Trofimovitch brings on his own death in rebelling against the domination of Mme Stavrogin ; in the younger generation Stavrogin commits suicide after rebelling against his exploitation by young Verhovensky. These two pairs and their inter-actions are the obverse and the reverse of the same coin : and obviously they can only be examined at one and the same time by splitting the coin, which is just what Dostoievsky did.

The simplest and clearest examples of the same technique, however, are in *Crime and Punishment* and *The Idiot*. In the former Raskolnikov and Svidrigailov, in the latter Prince Myshkin and Rogozhin, are complete and complementary antitypes to each other. They show how the simplest form of the process works. The qualities which are abstracted to form the characters of Svidrigailov and Rogozhin are those which can be grouped together under the title " demonic " : the insane rages, the murderous impulses, the frantic jealousy, the unmotivated changes of mind, the lawless will, the relent-less, self-torturing pride, and in general the whole *farrago* of instincts which psychology has relegated to the sub-conscious. But to call them demonic is not to suggest that they are abnormal ; on the contrary, there is no normal

[1] See above, p. 52.

human being altogether without them. The only peculiarity of Dostoievsky's treatment is that he deliberately isolates them for objective examination.

Yet the description of his technique is still not quite complete. For the study of character is not a static but a dynamic science : its subjects are in the process of becoming, not in the state of being. It is precisely because psychology requires the passage of time and the interaction of personalities through time as a background, that Dostoievsky's study of human character took the form of story-telling at all. A series of character-studies set in isolation would have been adequate to depict each of his mental creations at any given moment ; a fictitious biography (which is what many other novels are) would have been adequate to trace the development through time of one selected principal ; but only a novel that is a creative work of art could show the concurrent development through time of a large series of characters at once. Dostoievsky is thus unusual among novelists in that his characters are logically prior to his stories. The stories exist only as vehicles for the free development of the characters, who persistently take control of the narrative in a way which Dostoievsky admits without being aware that it is unusual.[1] In other words, his primary purpose was not to tell stories at all. It was to produce works of art in the dimensions available to a novelist. In this respect his only difference from other artists (who also may accidentally happen to tell stories) is that whereas a painter has only two dimensions at his disposal, and a sculptor three, a novelist has four : not only can his figures be created in the round, but they can move through time.

In the case of most novelists, this movement through time constitutes the whole substance of their narrative. They cut

[1] Cp. *The Possessed*, p. 57 : " it is not my fault if (the events) seem incredible." See also an early letter in Mayne, pp. 26-7.

a slab out of time that looks likely to make a good story, doing their best to carve it at the joints. That is not only how their novels come into existence : it is what they conceive a novel necessarily to be. But the reader of Dostoievsky must start by realising that this identification of a work of art with the efficient telling of a well-rounded story, however useful it may be in most cases, is purely fortuitous ; and the question what his stories are about is not, as in other novels, the first and only significant question, but the last and least significant. From the technical point of view he was not even a good story-teller. Mrs. Constance Garnett had often to tidy up his style in translation. His construction of plots is often amateurish ; his sense of chronology and consistency is demonstrably deficient ; his characters develop not only on different scales but at different speeds ; his narrative transitions were the laughing-stock of Russian critics for their crude ineptitude, and his climaxes were often dictated not by the progress of the action but by the exigencies of unplanned serialisation. On more than one occasion a character is given two separate introductions into the story ; [1] it is seldom possible to guess the time of year of the action ; and all too often the action is clumsily helped forward by *clichés* such as : " But something unexpected happened all at once. . . ." [2] These are the negative aspects of a comparative lack of interest in the external sequence of events. The positive aspect can be seen, for instance, in the skill with which Dostoievsky describes the setting in Petersburg of a dramatic tragedy with only one phrase of *physical* description in a whole paragraph ; [3] or in the extraordinary manner in which his characters develop through the chapters in the

[1] *E.g.* Lebyadkin in *The Possessed*, p. 25 *seqq.* and p. 352 : and Mme Hohlakov in *The Brothers Karamazov*, pp. 41 and 48.

[2] *The Idiot*, p. 84 and *passim*.

[3] *The Insulted and Injured*, p. 159.

reader's imagination even before their physical characteristics have been described at all.[1]

No more remarkable illustration of Dostoievsky's indifference to the external development of his narrative as such could be found than the passage in which, very late in *The Brothers Karamazov*, he introduces for the first time an account of Ivan Karamazov's attitude to his brother Dmitri with the casual preface : " By the way, . . ."[2] The significance of this is that it is indeed by the way. The internal development of both characters is already complete, and their relationship to each other is implicit in it, so that the reader is not taken by surprise at this new information, but is rather inclined to comment : " Yes, of course, that's right. . . ." This internal development of the characters during the course of the novels, even when they are not physically before the reader's attention at all, is the most powerful achievement of Dostoievsky's technique. It is like watching a play acted in the continental convention instead of the English : instead of leaving the characters who are not involved in the current dialogue to twiddle their thumbs in the background, Dostoievsky makes not only the *personae mutae*, but even those who are off the stage altogether, nevertheless steadily take part in the development of the story and of their own selves. What is Rogozhin doing while Prince Myshkin is talking to Aglaia ? Where is Nastasya while Ippolit is reading his pathetically absurd confession ? What are Prince Myshkin and Kolya thinking while they listen to it ? None of these questions are ever directly answered ; but their relevance is always implicit in the narrative, and the possibility of an answer to them (even if Dostoievsky cannot give it) is perpetually entailed by the progress of the novel.

[1] *E.g.* in *The Possessed* the colour of Mme Stavrogin's hair is only mentioned on p. 601, in the penultimate chapter.

[2] *The Brothers Karamazov*, p. 639.

This quality of *becoming* instead of *being* in Dostoievsky's characters is directly attributable to his preoccupation with the inner significance of events and characters rather than their outward manifestations. That preoccupation can be most vividly illustrated by two particular instances where Dostoievsky's personal stake in the physical manifestations was so vital and intense that his detachment in treating them is almost incredible. The first is Siberia : throughout the whole exhaustive account of the prison system, recorded from his own bitter experience in *The House of the Dead*, there is not the faintest flicker of criticism or moral disapproval, either of the crimes committed, or of the appalling suffering endured, or even of the injustice of his own condemnation. The second instance is epilepsy : in all the careful descriptions he gave, with the minute detail of personal recollection, of the symptoms and pathology of epilepsy,[1] there is never a hint of interest in the possibility of a cure, nor apparently did Dostoievsky in his own case ever seek a cure. The most characteristic of his comments on the disease is put into the mouth of Kirillov, describing the moment before an attack : [2]

There are seconds—they come five or six at a time—when you suddenly feel the presence of the eternal harmony perfectly attained. It's something not earthly—I don't mean it's heavenly—but in the sense that man cannot endure it in its earthly aspect. He must be physically changed or die. This feeling is clear and unmistakable ; it's as though you apprehend all nature and suddenly say, " Yes, that's right." God, when he created the world, said at the end of each day of creation, " Yes, it's right, it's good." It . . . it's not being deeply moved, but simply joy. You don't forgive anything because

[1] There are four principal examples : the little orphan in *The Insulted and Injured*, Prince Myshkin in *The Idiot*, Kirillov in *The Possessed* and Smerdyakov in *The Brothers Karamazov*.
[2] *The Possessed*, p. 537. Cp. *The Idiot*, pp. 219 *seqq.*

there is no more need of forgiveness. It's not that you love—
oh, there's something in it higher than love—what's more
awful is that it's terribly clear and such joy. If it lasted more
than five seconds, the soul could not endure it and must
perish. In those five seconds I live through a lifetime, and
I'd give my whole life for them, because they are worth it.

It is a comment of some importance on this profound passage
that Kirillov finally commits suicide, not in despair or
suffering, but as the supreme gesture of self-assertion.

Here is the kernel of Dostoievsky's thought and purpose
as a novelist. It lies in his comparative indifference to the
physical development through time of characters and events,
and in his preoccupation with the inner significance of the
universe. To Dostoievsky the inner meaning of things was
not merely more elevated or more profound or more noble
than their exterior : it was in the most literal and commonplace sense more *real*. Physical experiences such as epilepsy
or imprisonment were for him not things in themselves but
mere *phenomena* belonging to the world of " things as they
appear," [1] and therefore of secondary and derivative (but not
for that reason negligible) moment. Dostoievsky's concern
is with " things as they are apprehended by the mind," which
philosophers call " *noumena.*" In the external universe this
means that his primary interest may be called metaphysics ;
in the sphere of human conduct it can only be called by the
neologism, metapsychology. It is this penetration of his
thought beyond the phenomenal level that makes it possible
(and indeed inevitable) for him to record without emotion
the dumb and hideous suffering of the orphan child in *The
Insulted and Injured*, and without criticism the " incredible
delight " which Stavrogin felt in " every unusually disgrace-
ful, utterly degrading, dastardly and, above all, ridiculous "

[1] The term is borrowed from Kant's *Critique of Pure Reason*.

experience of his life ; [1] and to argue that if the physical pain of capital punishment were greater, the spiritual suffering would be less.[2] It is the same subordination of the phenomenal to the noumenal that accounts for the strange, morally disinfectant dialogue on prostitution between Raskolnikov and Sonia at the prostitute's bed-side ; [3] and for the paradoxical outburst of Dmitri Karamazov at his trial, when Katerina's earlier evidence had practically cleared him of the charge of murdering his father at the expense of betraying her own dishonour : " Katya, why have you ruined me ? . . . Now I am condemned ! " [4] Raskolnikov and Sonia were talking not of their bodies but their souls ; Dmitri Karamazov was thinking not of his father's murder but of his own right to spiritual suffering ; and Dostoievsky was writing not a " whodunnit " but a sublime interpretation of metaphysical truth.

Perhaps only in the New Testament (which was almost Dostoievsky's only reading for many years in Siberia) has anything superior to Dostoievsky's purpose and achievement, or anything at all comparable to it, been found. He was acutely aware of his affinity with the historical figure of Christ ; he wrote in a letter from Siberia : [5]

> If anyone could prove to me that Christ is outside the truth, and if the truth really did exclude Christ, I should prefer to stay with Christ and not with the truth.

His novels are permeated with a deep devotion to the Gospels, manifested not only in frequent quotation and in

---

[1] *Stavrogin's Confession, etc.*, p. 43.   D. H. Lawrence mistakenly wrote this off as " sinning your way to Jesus."

[2] *The Idiot*, p. 19.

[3] *Crime and Punishment*, pp. 281 *seqq*.   This theme originated in the second part of *Letters from the Underworld*.

[4] *The Brothers Karamazov*, p. 723.   [5] Mayne, p. 71.

the portraiture of both religious and irreligious figures, but especially in the imitation at a near remove of Christ's sublime genius for giving real expression to the noumenal world in the simplest of phenomenal terms and images. For this reason Dostoievsky was more at home with the apocalyptic interpretation of Christianity in the *Revelation* of St. John the Divine than with the rational interpretations of St. Paul.[1]   It is to St. John the Divine that the spiritual ancestry of Dostoievsky's religious thought can be traced ; and it is in the word " apocalypse " that the essence of his metaphysical technique is to be found.

[1] The *Revelation* is drawn upon extensively to justify a series of eccentric prophecies in *A Raw Youth* ; it is read by Stepan Trofimovitch on his deathbed in *The Possessed*, p. 594 ; and the one claim to consideration of Lebedyev in *The Idiot* is his supposed ability to expound its prophecies.

CHAPTER VI

APOCALYPSE

WHEN Dostoievsky is called a prophet, as he often is,[1] there are two quite distinct things that may be meant. One is a straightforward attempt to predict the future, like the Delphic oracle, Nostradamus or Old Moore. The other is the apocalyptic manner of writers like Isaiah, St. John the Divine or Blake. There are some writings which might be held simultaneously to fulfil both definitions : for instance, Virgil's fourth Eclogue, a piece of apocalyptic poetry which was, as it happened, rendered veridical *ex post facto* by the birth of Christ. Dostoievsky's work is a rare example of the fulfilment of both senses not simultaneously but separately.

The distinction between the two is easily defined. Prediction is either true or false ; apocalyptic writing is neither true nor false, but more or less significant. Prediction can only be recognised as veridical after the event. Apocalyptic writing is always recognisable as such from the moment it is written ; events only affect its significance in degree. A dual example is the twenty-ninth chapter of Isaiah : this was always an apocalyptic prophecy, but it was also turned into a veridical prediction by the siege of Jerusalem under Titus in A.D. 70. The same is true of Virgil's fourth Eclogue. But it is seldom true of Dostoievsky, in whose work prediction

---

[1] Or even *A Prophet of the Soul*, whatever that may be. It is the title of a book by Zenta Maurina (a Latvian), which is worth reading as a biography of Dostoievsky, like that by Stanislaw Mackiewicz (a Pole), for the viewpoint of some of Russia's nearest and most long-suffering neighbours.

and apocalypse become two separate functions that do not occur together. Prediction was a comparatively trivial matter to him, thrown off as a by-product. Apocalypse was his vocation.

Some of Dostoievsky's prophecies, though strictly predictive in relation to the accepted thought of his time, are no more than brilliant anticipations of trends that were already in progress. For instance, within a short time of the invention of photography, he pointed out the essential difference between a photographic and a painted portrait : [1] that whereas a photograph can only capture one mood at a time of the subject, a painting can synthesise any number of moods in an eclectic statement of character. He wrote this at a time when most artists regarded photography simply as a challenge to their ingenuity in precise reproduction. Later artists learned the lesson which Dostoievsky first pointed out, and photography became the release which enabled them to abandon naturalistic reproduction ; but so many have still not learned the lesson that for them (though they may never know it) Dostoievsky is still a prophet. In the same way, he was the first writer to foresee the possibilities of non-Euclidian geometry,[2] which had been pioneered a little earlier by the Russian mathematician Lobachevsky ; and the dangers of over-specialisation in medicine,[3] which have only been combated for the first time in the last decade by the evocation of the concept of " social medicine," to teach doctors to regard their patients as human beings with a place in society, instead of aggregates of pathological symptoms for the entertainment of specialists.

Medicine, including psychology and psychiatry, is naturally the field in which Dostoievsky's anticipations are most

[1] *A Raw Youth* (1916 edition), p. 456.
[2] *The Brothers Karamazov*, p. 240.
[3] *Op. cit.*, p. 679.

remarkable ; for although he was temperamentally indifferent to the possibilities of therapy, even for his own afflictions, nevertheless his meticulous interest in symptoms has provided specialists with case-material far in advance of his time. His works have been drawn upon for a monograph on tuberculosis [1] and for a study of the pathology and psychology of epilepsy.[2] The writers of the latter have particularly stressed that the only known formal psychologist whose works Dostoievsky had certainly read was the German Carus ; indeed, there were few others to be had at the time. The fact that Dostoievsky was born some half-century before Freud therefore makes all the more astonishing his anticipations in the field of sexual psychology. He might well be called the first psychoanalyst of exhibitionism (indecent exposure) and the Oedipus complex in *A Raw Youth* ; of adolescence and puberty in *A Little Hero* and *Nyetochka Nyezvanov* ; and of adult perversions towards adolescence in *The Possessed* (the suppressed chapter, published in England as *Stavrogin's Confession*) and in *Crime and Punishment*. To these examples can be added the study of split personality in *The Double* and elsewhere ; the presentation, both in *The Idiot* and in *The Insulted and Injured*, of a sexual passion irresolubly divided between two objects ; and most important of all, the study of dreams and hallucinations from the subconscious. In the pre-scientific age, of course, the interpretation of dreams was a matter of supreme importance ; but thereafter the early scientific age abolished it as superstitious ; and Dostoievsky was among the first to perceive its impending return in rational guise, which Freud was eventually to bring about. Practically all Dostoievsky's novels contain important

---

[1] Homero Silveira : *A Tuberculose na Vida e na Obra de D.* (Rio de Janeiro, 1948).
[2] S. S. Smith and A. Isotov : *The Abnormal from Within* (University of Oregon, 1935).

dreams, or hallucinations indistinguishable from dreams, and some of his short stories are called after them : for instance, *Uncle's Dream* (which was in fact not a dream) and *The Dream of a Ridiculous Man*. It is not surprising that Nietzsche referred to Dostoievsky as the one man from whom he had anything to learn in psychology ; [1] nor even that Freud convicted him of having an Oedipus complex himself. [2] But it is the testimony of Freud's great rival Adler that matters more, because Dostoievsky not only anticipated Freud in the study of the sexual instinct (in which thanks to Hollywood everyone has now caught him up) but also anticipated Adler in attaching primary importance in the motivation of human conduct to the instinct for power. This was something very new indeed, and still remains so in the Western world.

Adler was so impressed by Dostoievsky that he devoted a lecture to him in 1918, which concluded that " his achievements as a psychologist have not yet been exhausted." [3] In support of his judgment that Dostoievsky's " seer-vision penetrated deeper than the science of psychology," Adler quoted four examples of his anticipation of concepts which formal psychologists only reached after his day. The first was the significance of laughter (" the possibility of learning to recognise a man better from his laughter than from his life-attitude ") ; the second was the idea of " the accidental family, where every member lives for himself, isolated from the others " ; the third was " the origin of mental ailments in life as serving the purpose of revolt " ; and the fourth was " the tendency to despotism implanted in the human soul." The fourth is by far the most important. It was perhaps Dostoievsky's greatest discovery that sexual love,

[1] Nietzsche's Superman was partly anticipated by Raskolnikov in *Crime and Punishment*.

[2] In an essay called *Dostoievsky and Parricide*.

[3] *Individual Psychology*, p. 290.

even of the purest kind, contains among its elements the desire to exercise power over the beloved ; and if that desire is not gratified, love itself may come to contain hatred of one and the same object at the same time. This is the special theme of his short story, *A Gentle Spirit* ; but it is most profoundly expressed in the following passage, which he wrote of an engaged couple : [1]

> [He] set down these capricious impulses . . . to outbreaks of blind hatred for him, not due to spite, for, on the contrary, she esteemed him, loved him, and respected him, and he knew that himself—but from a peculiar unconscious hatred which at times she could not control.

The same preoccupation with the power-instinct accounts for Dostoievsky's fascination by the lowest forms of life : bugs, lice, slugs, worms and so on are often introduced, metaphorically to be crushed. The craving for power is also Dostoievsky's explanation of the suicide of the engineer Kirillov, in *The Possessed*, as the supreme act of self-assertion. The explanation might not be accepted by modern psychologists : for instance, Freud would have ascribed it to the emergence from the subconscious to the conscious mind of the " death-instinct," that is, the supposed *conatus* of all human beings to revert to an inorganic equilibrium. [2] But whether Dostoievsky was right or wrong, at least he was the first to pose a problem in apparently motiveless suicide, for which psychology has had to accept the challenge of finding an explanation.

In many of these matters Dostoievsky's mind was only moving ahead (though often a long way ahead) of other minds that were already on the same track. He was not for this reason the founder of modern psychology, any more than he was the founder of the Existentialist philosophy

---

[1] *The Possessed,* p. 302.   [2] See R. Fedden, *Suicide*, pp. 314–20.

merely because Sartre calls him the starting-point of some of its ideas.[1]　But there are two fields in which Dostoievsky's clairvoyance might legitimately have been written off as utter nonsense for nearly half a century, until events began to reveal their significance within the last generation.　One lies on the borderline between philosophy and science, the other on the borderline between philosophy and political action ; and what Dostoievsky did was to anticipate on the one hand some of the theories of psychical research, and on the other hand most of the revolutionary techniques of Communism.　The novelty of his vision in these two respects can be judged from two facts : in the one case that formal psychology, in which Dostoievsky was also a pioneer, has usually been the most determined obstacle to the scientific establishment of the phenomena of psychical research ; and in the other case that Dostoievsky's theory of revolution is at many points in direct conflict with the gospel of Marx, which has so uncritically been accepted as canonical.

Psychical research is no new thing, and the first known attempt at empirical verification of telepathy can be dated at the latest to the sixth century B.C. ; [2] but it is only within the last twenty years that the subject has been elevated by American practitioners to the status of a science, under the new name of para-psychology.　A recent summary of their work [3] shows that at least four distinct phenomena are involved : telepathy and clairvoyance, which are grouped together as extra-sensory perception (ESP) ; precognition ; and psycho-kinesis (PK), which may be picturesquely described as the exercise of control by mind over matter.　Recent research has established at least a strong probability that these

---

[1] *Existentialism and Humanism* (tr. Mairet), p. 33.

[2] Croesus' experiment on the Delphic oracle : see Herodotus' *History*, book I, chh. 46–8.

[3] J. B. Rhine, *The Reach of the Mind* (Faber, 1948).

four phenomena are all caused by the operation of a single human faculty, which has accordingly been called "psi" for short. The importance of all this for the biography of Dostoievsky is that every one of these phenomena occurs in his novels ; and that not as mere story-telling devices, or forced improbabilities introduced to create climaxes and resolve structural tangles, but as normal incidents in human life and conduct, intrinsic to the characters and narrative. In fact, any one of the relevant episodes might equally well have been a casual specimen from the case-book of one of the scientific investigators working on the problem more than half a century later.

The cases of extra-sensory perception (both telepathy and clairvoyance) and of precognition come mainly, but not exclusively, from The Idiot ; and they fall mainly, but again not exclusively, within the triangular relationship of Prince Myshkin, Nastasya and Rogozhin.[1] Thus, Myshkin finds himself intuitively guided towards Rogozhin's house when he is seeking it, though he has never been there before nor seen Rogozhin for several weeks (p. 198) ; he becomes conscious of Rogozhin's eyes watching him on four distinct occasions within one day, although only on the fourth occasion is Rogozhin present, and that is when he tries to murder Myshkin (pp. 225 seqq.) ; he predicts that Rogozhin will marry and murder Nastasya, when he has not yet met her but only seen her photograph (p. 33), and repeats the prediction to Rogozhin after his first attempt to marry her (p. 207) ; shortly before the murder takes place, exactly as he has predicted, he experiences a hallucinatory visitation from Rogozhin (p. 402) and at least one from Nastasya (p. 448). But Dostoievsky is at pains to show that these experiences are not connected with Myshkin's epilepsy or abnormality, nor are they all cases of awareness of abnormal

[1] See above, p. 49.

D.—7

phenomena.[1] They are not due to Myshkin's abnormality, because both Ippolit (p. 378) and Nastasya (p. 581) experience similar hallucinations of Rogozhin's presence ; and Myshkin has at least one precognition of a perfectly trivial event, which is that he will upset a vase at Mme Epanchin's tea-party (pp. 536-7). The most remarkable precognition in the story, moreover, is Nastasya's, in which she foresees the exact scene that is to follow her murder at the hands of Rogozhin, when her body will lie " wrapped in American leather . . . and surrounded with jars of Zhdanov's fluid " (pp. 447 and 598). The manner in which all these episodes are narrated, besides others that could be quoted from *The Possessed*, *The Brothers Karamazov* and elsewhere, are enough to suggest that Dostoievsky's work would at least repay examination by students of para-psychology as well as normal psychological phenomena.

More remarkable still, however, are the instances of the operation of the psi-faculty in the form of psycho-kinesis. Professor Rhine believes that this power has been established by his experiments with dice and other means subject to exact laws of average.[2] The only difference of Dostoievsky's " experiments," apart from the fact that they were conducted outside laboratory conditions and without adequate controls, is that he used the roulette-wheel in place of dice ; but the principle is the same. Moreover, Dostoievsky found, like Professor Rhine, that personal distractions reduced the effectiveness of the psi-faculty ; [3] that is why he always left his wife as far as possible from the scene of his experiments. It is also why his experiments all failed, because he was incapable of eliminating all the distractions, especially those natural to his own uncontrollable temperament. But in

[1] This conforms with Professor Rhine's observations : see especially *The Reach of the Mind*, Chapter 9, pp. 109 *seqq*.

[2] *Op. cit.*, Chapters 6–8.   [3] *Op. cit.*, pp. 101 *seqq*.

principle *The Gambler*, for instance, can be read from start
to finish as an essay in para-psychology ; and the theme also
shows its head in other works. The following passage deserves
to be regarded as a *locus classicus* on the subject : [1]

> . . . I still retain the conviction, that in games of chance,
> if one has perfect control of one's will, . . . one cannot
> fail to overcome the brutality of blind chance and to win. . . .

A similar passage is to be found at the very end of *The Gambler*,
where the narrator insists that at roulette " the great thing
is will power " [2] and quotes " a remarkable instance of
determination " which enabled him to start winning with the
last coin in his possession. In that case the effort of will was
apparently evoked by the challenge of desperation, just as
Professor Rhine argues that a challenge given to a subject
in para-psychology tests often produces better results ; and
that those who believe in the psi-faculty do better than those
who disbelieve.[3] In all this Dostoievsky was an intuitive
pioneer.

The last of Dostoievsky's major essays in predictive anticipation, which is that of revolutionary Communism, can be dealt
with more briefly, because the only way to study it at length
is by reading *The Possessed* from cover to cover.[4] The essential
point on which Dostoievsky was right and Marx was wrong,
however, can be stated simply : it was that revolution was to
be a national and not a supra-national phenomenon ; and
above all that it was bound to become religious, even if it
began by repudiating religion (p. 227). From this correct
premiss, Dostoievsky deduced a theory of revolution which
has proved right to the last particular in the generation since

---

[1] *A Raw Youth* (1916 edition), p. 278.
[2] *The Gambler*, pp. 131–2.   [3] *Op. cit.*, p. 120.
[4] See my article, " A Guidebook to Revolution," in *The Listener*,
27 October 1949.

1917. He foresaw that its inception would have nothing to do with the working class ; that it would rely on the ruthless discipline of an inner clique ; that it would deliberately rewrite history to glorify itself with legends ; that the " cement of the revolution " would be the compulsion to share in bloodshed (p. 351) ; that scientific socialism was logically unworkable (p. 226) ; and that the inevitable culmination of absolute equality must be in absolute slavery (p. 379). He depicted his leading revolutionaries as everything that they were in fact to be : the rootless aristocrat, the minor clerk, the romantic officer, the doctrinaire pedant, the educated ex-serf, the drunken buffoon, the convicted criminal, the impressionable adolescent, but never the worker ; he even gave one character, Shatov, a background recognisably similar to that of Zhelyabov, the organiser of the assassination of the Tsar Alexander II, although he could never have known Zhelyabov and had written *The Possessed* before his revolutionary career began.[1]

Perhaps the strangest single example of Dostoievsky's prescience in this respect is his exposure of the cell-system of conspiracy. He showed how the revolutionary hierarchy of small groups called " cells," in each of which only one man is in contact with the superior cell, could be abused to establish a cell which believed itself to be part of a gigantic organisation, although in fact it was the only one in existence. That is what Verhovensky organises in *The Possessed*, and it is never quite clear to his comrades whether or not he is in fact a conspirator or a police-spy all the time. A generation later, at the beginning of the twentieth century, exactly the same fraud was carried out by a notorious *agent provocateur* called Azev, whom no one could positively identify either as a

[1] The Tsar's minister, Pobedonostsev, congratulated Dostoievsky on the excellence of his portraiture of revolutionary types a few years later (*New D. Letters*, p. 82).

conspirator or as a spy. He was even made the subject of a novel called *What Never Happened*, written by Savinkov in 1912 ; but it might be argued that the crucial novel about him had already been written by Dostoievsky. What is most remarkable of all about this is that, although Dostoievsky saw through the whole façade of revolution and exposed its essential rottenness and evil, nevertheless he proudly asserted —and rightly, in contrast to Marx—that it was to spring from a characteristically Russian initiative.

It is at this point that Dostoievsky's vision passes over from prediction to apocalyptic mysticism. For in describing the technique of revolution he was simply stating with astonishing accuracy what was going to happen ; but in considering the theory of revolution, he was giving expression to his own *Weltanschauung* and the place of Russia in it. What was peculiar about his vision at this point was not that he foresaw revolution in terms of religion and nationalism, but that he regarded them all as Russia's special gift to the world. Russia, religion and revolution were for him inseparable, and each implied the other : they were the three R's of his philosophical code. He held them to be inseparable not only for himself and his fellow-countrymen, but for the whole world. For Russia already possessed the one true religion, to which other nations were only fumbling their way ; and revolution, though it must certainly start in Russia like everything new, was really what had to happen to the whole of the rest of the world in order to bring it into line with Russia. Such was Dostoievsky's view of the mission of Russia, the substance of his apocalypse.

The view was well grounded in history, though it was not commonly understood by Dostoievsky's contemporaries. It is not readily realised in the West, accustomed as it is to accepting top place in the world as a natural reward for its unique inheritance of Hellenism and Christianity, that the same unique inheritance (and therefore the same top place) was also divinely bestowed on Russia. Not only was Russia converted to Christianity from Constantinople, but also the legal inheritance of the Byzantine Empire could be argued to have passed to the Tsars when the niece of the last Emperor of Byzantium married Prince Ivan III of Moscow in 1472, after the fall of Constantinople. The Russian view of the situation was summed up by the monk Theophilus of Pskov in a well-known letter to the Grand Duke Basil III of Moscow, in which he described Moscow as " the third Rome, and a fourth there shall not be." Moscow was also spoken of as " the second Jerusalem," and most commonly of all as " Holy Moscow."

It is important that although this attribute extended from Moscow to all Russia, it never extended to Petersburg, which was founded by the first and most powerful of all Russian Westerners as a " window to the West." Peter the Great's new capital became the centre of all foreign influences in Russia, especially French and German. The German influence became particularly strong at the Tsarist Court, and German blood flowed in Tsarist veins. Petersburg was the natural point of entry from the West, especially after the opening of the Berlin–Petersburg railway in the 1850's. When Russia began to assert herself as a modern nation in the nineteenth century, however, there was at the same time a reaction against these influences. It was natural that those who so reacted should look back to Holy Moscow as their spiritual capital. Thus Moscow became the symbol of the Slavophils, and Petersburg of the Westerners. The difference between them in the intellectual controversy of the second half of the nineteenth century was roughly that the Slavophils regarded Russia as spiritually and materially self-sufficient, and the Westerners considered it more important to learn from the West and to assimilate Western techniques.

Dostoievsky held neither view, but a synthesis of the two. He was by birth a Muscovite and by adoption a Petersburger. His heart was in Petersburg, perhaps largely because Moscow was associated in his memory with the unhappiness of his school-days and his first marriage. On the other hand, what he saw of foreigners in Petersburg, and still more abroad, revolted him. With the exception of the English, whom he did not dislike as individuals, no foreigner cuts an agreeable figure in his writings :[1] Germans and Poles are almost invariably comic, Frenchmen and Jews almost invariably crafty rogues. The unforgivable offence of Turgenev in his eyes, even graver than his habit of being more highly paid than Dostoievsky, was his open acceptance of German nationality as preferable to Russian. This did not mean, however, that Dostoievsky accepted the reactionary autarky of the Slavophils. On the contrary, he asserted that Russia was of Europe not in the sense that Russia must learn of the West, but in the sense that the West must learn of Russia. This view may seem surprising to Western Europeans ; but it is worth remembering that to non-Europeans Russia looks just as much European as any other country ; and to many Asians Russia has long been (and is still more so to-day) the nearest and most impressive representative of Europe of all.

On the practical details of his Russian-born millenium, Dostoievsky was exceedingly vague : almost the only concrete prediction he formulated about it was that the Russians would reoccupy Constantinople, which still remains to be carried into effect. The special virtue of apocalyptic writing is that it can be made to mean practically anything, and even to reconcile flagrant contradictions. Thus, it is not clear whether Dostoievsky envisaged a pan-European war as a necessary and desirable step towards the fulfilment of Russia's mission

[1] Doctors were another exception : Swiss and German doctors figure attractively in *The Idiot*, *The Brothers Karamazov* and elsewhere.

or not. No one would suppose it who read his message only from the words of Father Zossima in *The Brothers Karamazov* ; no one would suppose anything else who read it only from the outpourings of *A Writer's Diary*. Father Zossima is the supreme expression of Dostoievsky's conception of Russia in terms of religion, as *A Writer's Diary*, written largely during the Slav uprisings against the Turks in 1875-7, is the supreme expression of his conception of Russia in terms of revolution. The need to reconcile his views in a single reasoned statement only came in the last year of his life, when he made his famous speech at the Pushkin festival on 8 June 1880. The result of the speech was temporarily to unite Westerners and Slavophils in a single seamless philosophy : it was a nine days' wonder, but no more. When the initial enthusiasm of the occasion wore off and people began to read what Dostoievsky had actually said, there seemed to be very little in it, and all the suspended controversies began again at the point where they had left off. The momentary triumph followed by the disillusioning aftermath was symbolically characteristic of Dostoievsky's general impact on the rational mind. He could evoke emotions, but he could not convince the intellect.

These are the strength and weakness common to all prophets. The consequence is their common fate, which is to be treated as all things to all people. Books have been written about Dostoievsky in many languages ; one day there may be as many books about him as about Shakespeare ; and all that are worth reading have found something new in him. He can be made the basis of a dissertation on capitalism [1] or on Christian apologetics ; [2] he reminds every critic of somebody or something quite different. To Spengler his was the voice, in contrast to Tolstoy's, of peasant Russia ; [3]

---

[1] O. Kaus, *D. et sa Destin* (French trans.).

[2] A. Zander, *Dostoievsky* (S.C.M. Press).

[3] *Decline of the West*, Vol. II, pp. 194-5.

to Kaus " il renie le paysan." [1]   To Berdyaev (a Russian) he
suggested Nietzsche (a German) ; to Nietzsche he suggested
Stendhal (a Frenchman), and to Kaus (another German) he
suggested Flaubert (another Frenchman) ; to Gide (a Frenchman) he suggested two Englishmen, Blake and Browning ;
to Mackiewicz (a Pole) he suggested among many others,
Thomas à Kempis ; and to many Englishmen he suggested
nothing on earth.   All these and hundreds of other
comparisons are perfectly valid, because Dostoievsky was a
universal genius ; none the less so for being an intensely
nationalistic Russian, just as Shakespeare was none the less so
for being wholly English.   He was a genius in the truest sense,
that he could tell us things which he did not know himself.

This, in one form or another, has been the conclusion of
all critics who have been able to step back from examining
the detail in order to see his achievement as a whole, especially
of those who have been creative writers themselves.   Tolstoy
wrote to Strakhov soon after his death, although he and
Dostoievsky never met : [2]

> How much I should like to be able to say all that I feel
> about Dostoievsky. . . . Suddenly, when he died, I realised
> that he was to me the man nearest, most dear and most
> needed. . . . At first I felt lost ; but then it became clear
> to me how dear he was to me, and I wept, as I weep now.

Gide wrote of him more explicitly : [3]

> *Il nous ouvre les yeux sur certains phénomènes, qui peut-être
> ne sont même pas rares—mais que simplement nous n'avions pas
> su remarquer.*

J. C. Powys was saying the same thing when he called
Dostoievsky a " psychic medium " ; [4] for the point about
his revelations is that even if the phenomena are not rare,

[1] O. Kaus, *op. cit.*, p. 246.   [2] *Anna*, p. 231.
[3] D. ; *Articles et Causeries*, p. 180.   [4] *Dostoievsky, passim.*

they are none the less ordinarily obscure and unintelligible, and the point about a medium is that often he does not himself understand what he is saying. This was often also true of what Dostoievsky had to communicate : it lay, in Wordsworth's phrase, "too deep for tears," much more for rational exegesis. How, then, this communication can be made, entailing as it does a transition from the noumenal down to the phenomenal world, is a great and impenetrable mystery ; for all the means of communication belong to the phenomenal world, and cannot bridge the gap. For Wordsworth the problem was solved by the meanest flower that blows ; for others, it is the peculiar prerogative of poetry. Very few novelists have succeeded in usurping this prerogative of poets, and Dostoievsky, alone among the Russians, is one of them.

The Russian novel is itself a remarkable phenomenon. It came into existence within Dostoievsky's own lifetime, and achieved sublime and mountainous heights before the end of the nineteenth century. Among the heights, Tolstoy's work is probably the loftiest single peak, and Turgenev's the greenest and most gracious single slope. Dostoievsky's work, on the other hand, is not a mountain but a whole range of mountains, massive, precipitous, perilous and unconquerable. It is a range whose summit has never yet been seen from below ; and anyone who climbs ambitiously up its foot-hills, confidently expecting to reach the top, finds that each peak which looks like the summit only conceals another one behind it. In his own time people could not even recognise that a mountain was before them, because it was too close ; it looked like nothing but a blank and shapeless obstacle. Now that we are at a distance from it, we are better able (if still only a little better) to estimate the magnitude of its vastness ; we are at least able to admit that its dimensions remain incalculable and its range unexhausted.

Men who first read Dostoievsky in their youth a generation ago, when he was first fully translated into English, have said of him that then they found the world he wrote of consistent and logical within its own logic, just like Alice's Wonderland, but quite mad by any ordinary standards ; yet now they realise that the world which Dostoievsky was describing is the world which we are living in. There is a sober warning in this. For the very marks by which they now identify it as our world are the same that seemed mad thirty years ago, and meaningless in Dostoievsky's own lifetime ; and there is much that still remains obscure to-day, awaiting a later generation to emerge into the light. Anyone who wants to know what the world is going to feel like fifty years from now could not do better than to re-read those passages of Dostoievsky (say, from *The Possessed*) which still seem to be most completely mad or unintelligible. One day they may seem to be neither. But there is no fixing a date when all Dostoievsky will stand revealed.

LIST OF WORKS

	Shorter Novels	Short Stories	Full-length Novels
1845–6	Poor Folk 1	A Novel in Nine Letters 4	
	The Double 2	Mr. Prohartchin 3	
1847	The Landlady 5	Polzunkov	
1848		A Faint Heart	
		A Christmas Tree and a Wedding	
		White Nights	
		An Honest Thief	
		Another Man's Wife	
1849	Nyetochka Nyezvanov	A Little Hero	
1850–9	(Imprisonment and exile in Siberia)		
1859	Uncle's Dream		
	The Friend of the Family		
	(Journalistic work for *Vremya* and *Epokha*)		
1861			The House of the Dead
			The Insulted and Injured
1862		An Unpleasant Predicament	
	(Journalistic work : *Winter Notes on Summer Impressions*)		
1864	Letters from the Underworld		
1865		The Crocodile	
1866	The Gambler		Crime and Punishment
1868			The Idiot
1869	The Eternal Husband		
1871			The Possessed
	(Journalistic work : *A Writer's Diary*, including short stories below)		
1875		Bobok	A Raw Youth
		The Peasant Marey	
1876–7		A Gentle Spirit	
		The Heavenly Christmas Tree	
		The Dream of a Ridiculous Man	
1880			The Brothers Karamazov

SELECT BIBLIOGRAPHY

The full bibliography of Dostoievsky would already be voluminous. These are only a few of the most useful books out of a large total. In certain cases which are frequently quoted in the text, the abbreviation used is given in brackets at the end of the title in this list. In all cases the novelist's name is abbreviated to an initial, to eliminate variations of spelling.

SOURCES

D. Portrayed by His Wife. Translated by S. S. Koteliansky. (Anna.)

D. : Letters and Reminiscences. Translated by S. S. Koteliansky. (Koteliansky.)

The Letters of D. to His Wife. Translated by Elizabeth Hill and Doris Mudie. (Hill and Mudie.)

Letters of Fyodor D. Translated by Ethel Colburn Mayne. (Mayne.)

New D. Letters. Translated by S. S. Koteliansky.

BIOGRAPHIES

E. H. CARR. *D., A New Biography.* 1931. (Carr.)

J. A. T. LLOYD. *A Great Russian Realist.* 1912.

J. MEIER-GRAEFE. *D., The Man and His Work.* Translated by H. H. Marks, 1928.

S. MACKIEWICZ. *D.* 1947. (Mackiewicz.)

S. SOLOVIEV. *D., His Life and Literary Activity.* Translated by C. J. Hogarth, 1916. (Soloviev.)

H. TROYAT. *Firebrand ; A Life of D.* Translated by N. Guterman, 1946.

CRITICAL STUDIES

N. A. BERDYAEV.   *D. : An Interpretation.*
A. GIDE.   *D. : Articles et Causeries.*
O. KAUS.   *D. et sa Destin.*   Translated from the German.
E. J. SIMMONS.   *D : The Making of a Novelist.*
S. ZWEIG.   *Three Masters : Balzac, Dickens, D.*

Other works are referred to in the text which did not seem of
sufficient general value to justify a place in this summary
bibliography.   It should be added that by far the most valuable
work for English readers is Professor E. H. Carr's biography,
which is likely to remain irreplaceable.

GENERAL INDEX OF PERSONAL NAMES

INDEX OF DOSTOIEVSKY'S FAMILY